DIFFICULT IDENTITIES

Every human being about to be born is loaned a provisional identity. This identity is embodied in the name they are given, as an invention, internal need, or generational obligation, parental fantasy or delusion. Both the person receiving and the person bestowing the name—and, with it, the provisional identity—are unaware of all this.

Interweaving theoretical reflections and clinical histories, Pia De Silvestris illustrates the dramatic nature, the profundity, and the cryptic complexity of the challenges posed by this difficult identity— challenges she has faced repeatedly throughout her psychoanalytic career. She sees the role of transference in psychic and relational life as a "continuous search for the origin", a force that develops continuously through a variety of exchanges and investments, which seek, on the one hand, to weaken the bond to the original object and, on the other, to preserve it until death. Throughout the book's chapters, we see how it is precisely the product of the transference experience that permits the joint work of identity construction to begin. Transference is always the outcome of an experience of fulfilment and an encounter with the other; and it is desire of the other that promotes the search for the self.

Pia De Silvestris is a psychotherapist who lives and practises in Rome. She is a full member of the Society for Psychoanalytic Psychotherapy for Children, Adolescents and Couples (SIPsIA) and the Italian Society of Psychoanalytic Psychotherapy (SIPP), and teaches on the training programmes of both societies. She has published widely in psychoanalytic journals, and has co-authored several books in Italian, among which are *Transference in Child Psychoanalysis* (1994); *Childhood Depression* (1997); *Transcribing the Unconscious* (2002); *Awareness and Self-Analysis* (2005).

"*Difficult Identities* is a vivid, vibrant, compelling collection of essays that makes for a unique psychoanalytic revisitation of the life cycle. With the sensitivity and acumen of the well-seasoned yet intrepid clinician whose psychoanalytic vision draws deeply on literature and the arts, De Silvestris brings influences as diverse as Kristeva and Bollas, Recalcati and Laplanche to bear fruitfully on her thinking and practice. What we have here is a series of distinctive chapters that together make for a most precise compass to help orient our understanding of, as well as our way through, the ongoing and relentless demands of what the author calls the work of identity."

Dr Anthony Molino, *psychoanalyst*

"In this poetic and thought-provoking book, the author reflects masterfully on the necessary psychic work that must be undertaken for a proper sense of identity to unfold. De Silvestris presents complex case material of children and adolescents to support her reasoning, while also describing how important it is for psychotherapists/analysts to lose their identity (at least for brief lapses of time) in order to establish contact with the psychotic and undifferentiated part of the patient. This is a book every psychotherapist should read."

Dr Alessandra Cavalli, *child and adult psychoanalyst*

DIFFICULT IDENTITIES

The Work of Identity in Human Life

Pia De Silvestris

Edited and translated by Sean Mark

LONDON AND NEW YORK

First published in English 2018
by Routledge
2 Park Square, Milton Park, Abingdon, Oxon OX14 4RN

and by Routledge
711 Third Avenue, New York, NY 10017

Routledge is an imprint of the Taylor & Francis Group, an informa business

Originally published in Italian in 2006 by
Edizioni Borla as
La difficile identità

British Library Cataloguing-in-Publication Data
A catalogue record for this book is available from the British Library

Library of Congress Cataloging-in-Publication Data
A catalog record has been requested for this book

ISBN: 978-1-78220-621-7 (pbk)

Typeset in Palatino
by The Studio Publishing Services Ltd
email: studio@publishingservicesuk.co.uk

CONTENTS

ABOUT THE AUTHOR

Pia De Silvestris is a psychotherapist who lives and practises in Rome. She is a full member of the Society for Psychoanalytic Psychotherapy for Children, Adolescents and Couples (SIPsIA), and the Italian Society of Psychoanalytic Psychotherapy (SIPP), and teaches on the training programmes of both societies. She has published widely in psychoanalytic journals, and has co-authored several books in Italian, among which are *Transference in Child Psychoanalysis* (1994); *Childhood Depression* (1997); *Transcribing the Unconscious* (2002); *Awareness and Self-Analysis* (2005).

NOTE ON THE TRANSLATION

When gender has not been specified and is not influential, I have varied the use of she and he. When the author quotes from works that have not been previously translated into English, I have translated from the original Italian or French for this edition.

For Alida and Adamo

PREFACE

Maria Luisa Algini

Growing up, our whole lives seem to stretch out before us. We make plans for the future, change our minds again and again. We might want to be an archaeologist one day, an astrophysicist the next, a historian, engineer, or writer the day after that. We consider following in our father's footsteps, or our mother's, or doing it all our own way. During childhood and adolescence, omnipotent fantasies of being able to change future plans over and over and again provide one of the strongest incentives to discover the resources we possess. These fantasies, in themselves, also constitute a very pleasurable game, putting our thoughts and emotions to the test.

When a child is in difficulty, however, such fantasies and plans become impossible. This is the case for Silvia, Roberto, Lucia, Nadia, Marco, Andrea, and Rosy—some of the characters we encounter in this book, and who capture our attention at once. They are children and adolescents like thousands of others, who appear well integrated in their school and social lives but are, in fact, hindered by an enigmatic internal object whose nature they cannot comprehend. They are gripped by states of panic and intellectual inhibition, tormented by compulsive washing or uncontrollable eating habits (or a terror of eating, with ensuing anorexia), or afflicted by premature losses that have extinguished their hopes and dreams. At best, their plans for the future resemble a kind of magical thinking that turns in on itself, and which can precipitate the descent into depression, hindering the child's progress rather than encouraging it. The child's capacity to dream her future is only one of the markers of profound (and imperceptible) internal processes. Indeed, in the simplifying ways in which infants and adolescents regard their identity, sense of self is bound to what they concretely *do*. What they do, however, is predicated upon very different functions.

In this valuable and engaging book, Pia De Silvestris focuses on the tragedy of this invisible imprisonment, which she neatly labels *difficult identity*. With great clarity and sensitivity, she explores the core of suffering that leads children, teenagers, and young adults to seek psychoanalytic treatment as a last resort to put their development back on track, to recover its meaningfulness and pleasure.

"We don't understand him any more," parents often say, in the first consultation, to express their children's difficulties as well as their own confusion. "I can't understand myself any more," say young adolescent patients, "I don't know what's happening to me." These are the terms they use to voice the malaise that children express through symptoms, extravagant or hyperactive behaviour, unhappiness, or mental blocks. The words express our necessity to know our needs and desires, to salvage them from the spirals of repetition, blind spots, ineptitude, and self-destructiveness, but also allude to something that is difficult to define, linked to the possession of a secret something that makes us feel unique. It is this unique something that allows us to make of our lives an unmistakable sign belonging solely to us. This makes me think of Christopher, the autistic protagonist of Mark Haddon's novel, *The Curious Incident of the Dog in the Night-Time*. After his mother explains his name's biblical origin to him, he says,

> Mother used to say that it meant Christopher was a nice name because it was a story about being kind and helpful, but I do not want my name to mean a story about being kind and helpful. *I want my name to mean me.* (2012, p. 20)

This idea of a singular correspondence of identity is reflected in the evocative fairytale that concludes De Silvestris's book, *The King and the Flute Player*. It tells the story of a king's frantic search for the mysterious song he has heard only in his dreams, a song that resonates deeply with his soul, but which he cannot find again.

Throughout the book, De Silvestris illustrates the dramatic nature, the profundity, and the cryptic complexity of the challenges posed by this difficult identity—challenges that she has faced during her many years working as a psychoanalyst. We read in the first chapter,

> Every human being about to be born is loaned a provisional identity. This identity is embodied in the name he or she is given, as an inven- tion, internal need, or generational obligation, parental fantasy or delusion. Both the person receiving and the person bestowing the name—and, with it, the provisional identity—are unaware of all this.

One interpretation could be that, at the beginning of our lives, we receive a potential inheritance from our parents through our primary relationships. This inheritance, both conscious and unconscious in nature, is made up of profound identifications, innate or acquired abilities we might or might not pursue, and the restrictions and opportunities resulting from our environment. It might provide an asset for future fruitful investments or be a cumbersome, paralysing burden—even a destructive compulsion.

All this may be clearly observed in clinical work with children, adolescents, and parents. Every child has her own way of coming into possession of the psychic inheritance she receives, and must transform it to make it her own. The cost of such an operation is unavoidable for parents and children alike, and symptoms are almost always the expression of the child's difficulties in finding a way out.

De Silvestris has been working on these complex matters—in which many factors, both internal and external, come together—for many years. First, in the early 1980s, when we trained together at the Society for Psychoanalytic Psychotherapy for Children, Adolescents and Couples (ASNE-SIPSiA), one of the first schools of psychotherapy for the developmental age founded by Adriano Giannotti, Professor of Child Neuropsychiatry in Rome, and Doctor Andreas Giannakoulas from London's Tavistock Clinic, then in research carried out in various study groups, which led to several publications, in the years of her SIPsIA Presidency (1995–1999), and now as a teacher on the centre's psychotherapy course.

The central role of transference in psychic and relational life is a common thread in De Silvestris's work. She sees it as a "continuous search for the origin", a force that develops continuously through a variety of exchanges and investments, which seek, on the one hand, to weaken the bond to the original object and, on the other hand, to preserve it until death. Throughout the book's chapters, we see how it is precisely the product of the transference experience that permits the joint work of identity construction to begin. Transference, writes the author, is always the outcome of an experience of fulfilment and an encounter with the other, and desire of the other promotes the search for the self. This is evident in the difficult case histories that this book presents. Analysis is the construction of a new internal history, but this entails a journey through what is often rough and risky terrain.

Identity—and especially gender identity—is a topic on which much is written nowadays, in both sociology and in psychoanalytic literature. It seems important, therefore, to draw attention to the author's particular point of view. To use an analogy, De Silvestris speaks of identity as a kind of magnet, which operates in the depths, and guides the child or adolescent to containing and bearing within herself an array of conflicts. These conflicts might include the illusion of being bound to the original matrix and the disillusionment of feeling separated from it, confronting oedipal vicissitudes by articulating childhood experiences, but keeping them suspended in a latency position, or the work needed to integrate psychically the image of a pubertal body. "Identity", writes De Silvestris in the first chapter, "is made up of those portions of the ego that are identified with the experience of an adequate correspondence between internal and external reality, and, therefore, do not have to be subjected to repression or splitting".

The book draws out a trail for the construction of identity over the arc of development, in a manner unlike any we might find in textbooks on the developmental age. It offers, instead, something a little like a map, helping us navigate a big city we are unfamiliar with; it does not send us down precise roads, but gives us general directions; it does not prescribe this or that mode of transportation, but tells us the places where we must stop off, turn around, change course. These turning points include the omnipotence at the beginning of every life and the necessity that this omnipotence come to an end, giving way to the darkness of loss but also entry into the real, the exclusivity of the relationship with the mother, and a new structuring mediated by oedipal tensions, the suspension of the latency position, to accommodate the child's ambivalence between dismissing and preserving the parental bond, and the long and difficult path of adolescence.

The book explores many different facets of adolescence, a crucial period for identity dynamics. "The fundamental characteristic of the adolescent mind", De Silvestris writes in Chapter Six,

> is that, in becoming aware of the power of its functioning, it recognises itself in the present, and appropriates both its past and the possibility to plan its own future. This is the typical functioning of a mind that works on two fronts, located on a strategic perspective to control and administrate two powerful psychic forces—the force aiming to confuse, and the force aiming to separate. We could say that, side by side, the death drive and life drive look toward life.

Though we may outline stages and sequences in the construction of a difficult identity, the process certainly does not resemble the construction of a building, where brick follows brick, floor follows floor. She continues, "One of the difficulties of psychoanalytic observation consists in distinguishing precisely and clearly between more primitive and more sophisticated or secondary levels of functioning, and assigning them to each developmental phase. In the reality of clinical practice, these diverse levels of functioning always appear and find expression at the same time".

*   *   *

Another key aspect of the book is the very effective way theoretical reflections alternate with clinical histories. It is quite evident that these theoretical reflections result from clinical practice, but also that, in each chapter, the case histories follow the theory to shed light on the thinking that helped shape them. Some histories, in particular, elicit a great deal of curiosity. What went on, we ask ourselves, as the deep core we call identity slowly took shape inside the patient? What type of interpretation or verbalisation of needs, desires, libidinal or destructive objects occurred in the here and now of the therapeutic relationship? How, in short, was the analyst able to help that child or adolescent effectively?

In a telling passage in Chapter Six, the author clarifies her psychoanalytic position. "A subject whose identity is still immature needs a therapist with a solid identity", she writes, someone who has confidence in the therapeutic method and does not need to be found and used as an object straightaway. I would say that the most favourable environment is one in which the therapist can wait and support the adolescent patient . . . When patients have had a sufficiently reliable experience of a non-competitive relational setting, which does not predefine their identity, they will then begin to transfer aspects of the self, aspects of relationships that have not yet been integrated, and repudiated part-objects. Only then will they begin to acknowledge their own needs and desires, on the one hand, and the qualities of the object, on the other. It is at this point that the real analytic work begins.

In line with these remarks, the author focuses mainly on the analyst's mental attitude in the various moments of the relationship and on the web of thoughts that might constitute a holding for the child's germinal self. In this regard, another important aspect of this book is its conjunction of Freud and Winnicott, a link that is seldom explicated in psychoanalytic literature. Indeed, Winnicott's theories are quite often presented without clarifying their relationship to the Freudian precedent—is he correcting, integrating, or ignoring Freud? Or is he saying something entirely different?

De Silvestris, who has a thorough knowledge of the writings of both authors, but is also conscious of didactic needs, highlights the ways in which Winnicott develops Freud's concepts (which lose insight and prominence if we ignore their Freudian origin). Good examples of this are: "According to Freud, thought ensues from the frustration of the object's absence; for Winnicott, life—that is, the acknowledgement of the object's absence—is possible only if there has been a prior experience of the object's presence", and

In the *Project for a Scientific Psychology* (1895), Freud speaks of the concept of *Hilflosigkeit* (the infant's helplessness) . . . and in *The Future of an Illusion* (1927c), he links the need for illusion with human desire. Subsequently, Winnicott renders illusion a theoretical construct to found the potential for psychic relations.

Evidently, without Freud there would be no Winnicott, and, as the author notes, Winnicott does not need to cite Freud continuously, having profoundly assimilated his writings. As in the complex case of personal identity, successful intellectual filiation does not need to cite its origins continuously, but can show the fecundity of its lineage by giving rise to a new theoretical identity.

Reading this stimulating and rigorous book, packed full of original clinical and theoretical ideas, I was reminded of Freud's response to Jung, in a letter dated 27 August 1907, on the subject of personality (a concept closely linked to identity): "I mean that these are concepts drawn from surface psychology and we in metapsychology are beyond them, although we cannot yet replace them from inside" (McGuire, 1974, pp. 79–80). When it comes to identity, too, we always seem to linger somewhere "beyond", as if in constant pursuit of its most defined form, which escapes us theoretically but which we can clearly grasp internally, both because we experience a part of it and continually search for its wholeness.

Reading De Silvestris's book also brought to my mind Jorge Luis Borges's short story "Blue Tigers", in which the protagonist searches for these mysterious animals in a remote village in India. He will discover that these blue tigers are not, in fact, animals, but mysterious "stones that spawn", whose "shape is that of the moon when it is full, and [whose] colour is the blue that we are permitted to see only in our dreams" (2011, p. 111). These disturbing stones increase and decrease in size, multiply, disappear, and reappear following completely irrational logic. The protagonist is terrified and shocked by the discovery of such disorder at the very heart of the order governing his life; in the end he can find no other solution than to get rid of these disturbing objects. The charm and distinctiveness of De Silvestris's book is that it acquaints us with the reverse process, allowing the inconstancy of experience—which is always new and often destabilising—to co-exist within us with a persistent core that is ours alone. The difficult identity, as defined by the author, is also our ability to inhabit our conflicts as an essential condition of life.

Introduction

Maurizio Balsamo

Some books move us with the beauty of the writing, the complexity of thought, the feelings they stir up. It is with great pleasure that I present such a book to the Anglophone reader. Its author, Pia De Silvestris, is a child and adolescent analyst who is very well known in Italy, particularly for the personal style of her writing and her ability to get straight to the heart of the matter. Her work offers novel perspectives and explores ways of thinking and feeling, relational devices and attitudes, that are capable of engaging psychotic states, conditions of unusual suffering, and mortification of the soul.

I have known De Silvestris and her work for many years, and have witnessed, in our professional exchanges and conversations, just how rich her inner, cultural, and relational worlds are. She is equally at home discussing painting, cinema, poetry, and art, in an admirable and eminently readable way. She shows great clinical experience, profundity, and humanity in her writing and this book, in particular, is both a high point of her professional development and a useful tool for future generations of analysts and analysts in training.

As we progress through the book, we find ourselves rereading with pleasure certain passages, striking intuitions, and conceptions of analysis that bespeak the author's immense and established experience, both personal and psychoanalytic. In one such key passage, De Silvestris gives her take on the question of identity, which she understands as those portions of the ego that are

> identified with the experience of an adequate correspondence between internal and external reality, and, therefore, do not have to be subjected to repression or splitting, but can, instead, easily be joined up by this identity. It is precisely this same portion of ego that can perform an analytic and auto-analytic function.

Reflecting briefly on this fundamental premise, we may deduce some relevant preconditions for analytic work.

1. Identity is not a genetic entity, pre-existing the subject's experience in time—a sort of biological and pre-linguistic incipit, as some French authors argue (I am thinking, here, for example, of Michel de M'Uzan). It is, instead, the product of an encounter between internal and external realities, between the subject and the environment, which is encoded according to the pleasure principle. (Naturally, more primitive traces, such as, for example, pictographic configurations, may also be included.) Accordingly, I am (and take inside myself) all the goodness that the world offers me in satisfying my drive-related needs, and such relational vicissitudes and oscillation of states of wellbeing, define the general *form* in which later states and experiences are encoded. It is this state of constancy (sameness) that institutes a particular configuration within the psychic apparatus, unaltered by splitting and repudiation of psychic content.

2. (Here her perspective strikes me as original.) The author reclaims the concept of "identity" within psychoanalytic theory (which speaks more willingly of identifications than identity). Identity here becomes the premise of self-analysis and the analytic function, understood as the possibility that states of being analyse other states of being, in a recursive dynamic that permits original states to be inscribed and reinscribed through transformations. Without this fundamental encounter, the analytic function cannot develop. In her case histories, De Silvestris accordingly shows how terror, anxiety, or disintegration are, in a certain sense, anti-analytic functions that need to be made good, to permit the constitution of a continuous identity on to which the analytic function can be grafted.

3. Instead of being a hindrance to the analytic process, identity, therefore, becomes that which permits it—a primary relational encounter stable enough to accommodate the openness and subjective deconstruction of analytic work.

4. Furthermore, identity cannot be conceptualised without taking into consideration the matter of transference. Indeed, transference is, in itself, rooted in the primary search for an external object able to satisfy internal needs, so that the created/found object can be internalised. It is precisely when this occurs that the subject can open himself to life and development. Likewise, if there is transference at the beginning, it is only within the transference that this primary state and relationship can be re-thought, re-transcribed, reworked, or staged again. (Thus, it becomes clear why it was precisely traumatic neurosis that led Freud to reformulate the analytic cure.) Indeed, if this origin is organised around a traumatic core (a "destiny"), it is often this traumatic core that organises the subject's sense of being, offering a terrain to cling to in order to avoid being overwhelmed. Trauma is not only the subject's history, but also his own original narrative; it becomes the very fabric of existence, which conveys meaning and individuality, albeit paradoxically.

De Silvestris's work and research aptly show how essential it is to respond to the basic human need for existence, continuity, and thinking, so that meaning can be created. The author puts to work the concepts of the original traumatic nuclei, the challenge they pose to analytic work, and how they can be transformed and expand knowledge about oneself and the other. Essentially, as the author writes, evoking Freud, the primary aim of the living being is "to tolerate life". Tolerating life implies many things: a certain acceptance, of course, but also, and above all, establishing the conditions under which the subject can appropriate her own history and experiences, however best she can. This is achieved by learning how to bear a modicum of psychic pain rather than by resorting to destructiveness or self-destructiveness as a way of expelling it. If it is true that one cannot change or forget one's origin, because it is repeated in all our experiences, it is also true that by reworking it—in the works of transformation and displacement—there is room for development. In a sense, identity ends up being the movement, to and fro, between the origin and its transcriptions, between the origin and its metamorphoses. But what seems even more interesting to me, in this perspective, is that if we think of the origin as a search for correspondences, similarities determined by an at least partial coincidence of internal states and responses of the object, then this origin can be conceptualised as what provides the momentum for the work required to give a subjective form to one's life through acceptable, progressive approximations. Winnicott's theory of the created/found object is already present in the subject's search for a correspondence, which can only find what is found (i.e., an Other, which can then be taken in within the subject). In essence, therefore, identity proves to be an appropriation of relational vicissitudes, something not unlike when children say "it's mine" of an object that does not belong to them, imitating its legitimate owner. Identity, we might say, is an uninterrupted effort to appropriate otherness.

These short observations do not do justice to the manifold interests of Pia De Silvestris's book. The author shows a continuous ability to develop every argument—whether culled from theoretical reflections or the consulting room—to shed new light, to show that even the more despairing forms contain, hidden or waiting, a hope of finding or re-finding meaning. This is not simply a question of an optimistic attitude, or the primacy of Eros, which must also obviously play a role in the analytic stance, but, rather, the direct consequence of a theory coherently based on the significance of the relationship. If the object is there from the beginning, and even when it has left destructive traces, what remains is the indelible *form* of the search for an object that goes from A to B, that initial drive that preserves its own memory, even when it presents itself as a memory of denial, rejection, and murder. At the beginning there has, in any case, been a dim awareness of the other in the relationship, whether in terms of love, thought, or regard, or in the denial of these things. The content of this first search for an object certainly makes a difference, determining subjective wellbeing or malaise, and accounts for adolescent manifestations of infantile sexuality, as a difficult or impossible *reprise* of what has not yet been represented or is unrepresentable. The subject might not replicate psychic contents that have never reached representation, but reproduces the mode with which she is searching for her own identity and origins. This is what becomes available for the work in the transference; indeed, analytic work concentrates on the subject's way of functioning rather than the contents of this internal world.

De Silvestris explains this concept very well when she writes that "Conceptualising transference as a return to the origin, the function of the analyst does not only consist in recognising the transference [what we might call "content analysis"], but also in eliciting and organising it". In this way, she establishes a double vector, particularly evident in child analysis, that combines, on the one hand, the need to give meaning to experiences and, thus, to the self, with the necessity to trace out a path that permits a constant return to the origins, to rediscover the illusion of continuity enabling us to set out again on a new journey. It is quite clear, then, that this theorisation departs from other models established for child analysis (and not only) that privilege the here and now or the present of the analytic relationship. The relationship and history—time present and time past—come together in a theoretical model that regards the relationship as a manifestation of the origin, while also regarding the origin as a resistance or constraint, a condition of feasibility, or a way of shaping the relationship in the present. Every form, as Freud writes, is the precipitate of more primitive contents; conversely, new content *can become form*.

To conclude, I would like to think that reading this book can be enlightening not only for its intrinsic value, but also as an illustration of the maturity of Italian psychoanalytic thought, of which—as I have said—De Silvestris is an extraordinary exponent.

CHAPTER ONE

Difficult identity

At the origin, and as far as can be presently observed, every human being about to be born is loaned a provisional identity. This identity is embodied in the name he or she is given, as an invention, internal need, or generational obligation, parental fantasy or delusion. Both the person receiving and the person bestowing the name—and, with it, the provisional identity—are unaware of all this.

Whether this identity is a potential asset or an advance to be paid on the price of life is also unclear. What is certain, however, is that even when the latter is true, many people are able to go on to harness this potential identity as an asset and develop the potential contained therein. Indeed, perhaps the individual's lot might hinge precisely on his ability to recognise this price to pay and, consequently, to take possession of it, as well as its potential for investment. Since this price must be paid in pain, however, any attempt to avoid such pain also prevents the recognition of what is truly at stake, and this scenario precludes any possible inheritance, whatever this might be. It is, of course, impossible to define all the scenarios that occur, and the ways they come to pass, from a psychoanalytic perspective, but the idea can be taken as a provisional stimulus for reflection and investigation, and then developed in clinical practice.

In her book, *Il viaggio con i bambini nella psicoterapia* [The Psychotherapeutic Journey with Children], Algini writes,

> With children, psychotherapy becomes the place in which—in a shared situation and through the complex interplay of new representations and "theories" which continuously form and reform—the infant mind may establish continuity or discontinuity in the secret spaces shared with the parents.

"In other words", she explains, "psychotherapy creates a web of internal connections that can allow us to not be engulfed by the histories of those who precede us, and to use their precedent to begin to build our *own* history" (2003, p. 78, translated for this edition). Since our *own* history can be constructed only through our experience of the other (an experience that cannot be completely verbalised, and is perceived but not conscious), all constructions that unfold as the analytic relationship progresses concern moments of identity and mourning that are, so to speak, provisional, but indicate the many intermediate stages in the transformation of human psychism.

Ultimately, the possibility of carrying out analytic work is linked to the mind's capacity to suspend the acquisition of thought, judgement, and definition. This is a bit like repeatedly leaping into an apparent void—the void of the mind, the unknown opposed to the known. Paradoxically, however, this is only possible when the mind feels sufficiently anchored to secondary thinking; only then can it afford to question its provisional identity—that is, when this identity is rendered stable precisely by this anchoring, and, therefore, contains what Aulagnier calls symbolic "points of certainty" (2001, p. 108). I prefer to call this a "provisional identity", however, because the process of knowledge, which makes use of this analytic capacity, continuously transforms our identity—that is, the fleeting outcome of psychic work. Understood in its Freudian sense, this work should be carried out through the transcription and mediation of reality—articulated, in turn, as both recognition of unconscious content and the needs entailed, and as realisation of forms of ego satisfaction or defence.

For these reasons, if this work of analysis, cognition, and construction of identity finds itself facing an excessive conflict and is able to fulfil a symbolic identification, this is never purely symbolic, but also contains aspects of idealising or delusional identification. This would, therefore, suggest that even Aulagnier's "points of certainty" and identity's solid base remain provisional, in the sense that the possibility for transformation or becoming less alienable at a different stage of life remains. Instead, I would add (in agreement with Aulagnier) that all analytic functions pertain to the ego, not only in the case of conscious operations or movements, but also when we are unaware of the psychic work being done.

I believe that identity is made up of those portions of the ego that are identified with the experience of an adequate correspondence between internal and external reality, and, therefore, do not have to be subjected to repression or splitting, but can, instead, easily be joined up by this identity. It is precisely this same portion of ego that can perform an analytic and auto-analytic function. At the same time, the analytic function surely widens the scope of identity, providing the possibility for the ego to acquire new certainties from the experience of the relationship between the self and the other. In fact, many histories of suffering are built up and coagulate around a core of infantile trauma which, real or phantasmal, ends up becoming a cornerstone of the subject's way of being and relating to the world. Even if this core— which naturally depends on family environment and genealogy—is a source of suffering, we must not forget that it is also the only possible form of life the child can receive, and is used and transformed, as much as it can be, by the infant. In this sense, the primary object is not only given but also transformed by the relationship with the infant; in fact, each traumatic core adheres so strongly to one's perception of oneself that in order to be transformed, a considerable processing of loss and mourning must take place.

Originating, therefore, in an initial negative image of the self, the difficulty of constructing subjectivity should be seen as a difficulty calibrating needs and desires with reality. This is what I attempt to portray through the case histories of my patients, focusing on the use these children, adolescents, or young adults are able to make of their experiences of the mother, father, or their absences or losses, to piece together a troubled path toward an intimate sense of identity. If primary identification always calls the mother or maternal stand-in into question, the development of subjectivity must necessarily also take into account a third party, separate from the mother–child relationship. This is widely considered the function of the father. For

Freud, the paternal figure is decisive in psychological development due to natural rivalry with the son—a structure reconstructed through the myth of Oedipus. For Winnicott (1965[1960]), the father is prefigured by identification with the mother, with the mother as bearer of a paternal ideal, be this a husband-like, fatherly, symbolic, or ideal figure. In any case, this function still prepares the subject through an infinite series of illusory and omnipotent mediations of thought, which, by protecting the ego's fragile formation, make it possible to establish a relationship with the world and reality.

CHAPTER TWO

Interminable illusion

If a good narcissistic experience is essential to surviving the caesura of birth, we could say that the causation of all suffering resides in the adventures and misadventures of the early core experiences. While Freud regarded the caesura of birth as the foundation of psychic life, Winnicott made the significant discovery of the developmental vicissitudes of these early sufferings, their specific forms of expression, and possible transformations. According to Freud, thought ensues from the frustration of the object's absence; for Winnicott, life—that is, the acknowledgement of the object's absence—is possible only if there has been a prior experience of the object's presence and emotional participation. If the core issue is the caesura of birth, with its complementary urgent need to stave off the attendant separation anxiety, only the illusion of the continuity of the bond with the object can alleviate this wound.

Illusion and disillusionment are two aspects of the same vital process, while disappointment points to the interruption of such process. It is universally acknowledged that life would be unlivable without the ubiquitous presence of illusion; paradoxically, however, if we were unable to bear disillusionment, we would be exposed to a premature death. The lack of a satisfactory early experience of illusion, as well as a sudden premature disillusionment, always ensue in identity crises, or that specific form of suffering nourished by disappointment that melancholia essentially is, with the attendant implication of an impossible work of mourning. The articulation of these diverse layers of experience and alive relationships makes for a more or less pathological or satisfactory development with its oscillations of integration and splitting.

In the *Project for a Scientific Psychology* (1895), Freud speaks of the concept of *Hilflosigkeit* (the infant's helplessness), thus implicitly positing the necessity of illusion, and in *The Future of an Illusion* (1927c), he links the need for illusion with human desire. Subsequently, Winnicott renders illusion a theoretical construct to found the potential for psychic relations, in as much as it provides the basis for the vital transformation of the primary agonies of the beginning of life. Winnicott regards illusion and disillusionment as relational concepts, therefore not really comparable with intrapsychic experiences, because, in the context of a relationship, the illusory experience of omnipotence has a structuring and developmental function. This is unlike omnipotent states, which are usually cut off from relationships and represent a defence from the drives, and, thus, often take on a pathological function.

In "Primitive emotional development" (2001a[1945], p. 152), Winnicott writes,

> The baby has instinctual urges and predatory ideas. The mother has a breast and the power to produce milk, and the idea that she would like to be attacked by a hungry baby. These two phenomena do not come into relation with each other till the mother and child *live an experience together*. The mother . . . produces a situation that may with luck result in the first tie the infant makes with an external object, an object that is external to the self from the infant's point of view.
>
> I think of the process as if two lines came from opposite directions, liable to come near each other. If they overlap there is a moment of *illusion*—a bit of experience which the infant can take as *either* his hallucination *or* a thing belonging to external reality.

The "bit of experience" gives way to the construction of the intermediate area, in which transitional objects come into being and the experience of reality is possible only if it originates from illusion. The intermediate area is the creation of the drive to live, which registers the absence of the object as perception of absence, frustration, and lack, intertwined with the desire to make it good. Winnicott calls this "bit of experience" illusion—even if it is essentially reality-based—because it is, nevertheless, subjective reality, which, in the effort to re-establish the condition prior to the absence, creates the illusion of undoing the loss, thereby mastering it by creating it gradually rather than enduring it passively. "This illusion", write Hernández and Giannakoulas (2003, p. 101, translated for this edition), "provides the child with a protective retreat, but does not isolate him".

The end point of the process of disillusionment is the attainment of the capacity to acknowledge the absence of the object, and the understanding, which is its corollary, that the object belongs to the external world. If illusion—the overlap between what the mother provides and what the baby imagines it to be (Winnicott, 2005a)—permits the human being to postpone facing the anxiety of being a separate individual, disillusionment helps us become aware of our separate existence.

While Freud sought a dynamic equilibrium between our need for illusion to deal with our finitude and the boundaries of our subjective identity, and the importance of disillusionment for drive development, Winnicott focuses his attention more on the developmental function of disillusionment and on the psychic risk of a premature disruption of illusion. Pontalis (1981) argues that the analytic setting seeks to actualise the area of illusion. He quotes from Marion Milner's description of transference as a "creative illusion", fundamental to psychoanalytic technique, through which a better adaptation to the world within and without is developed.

Silvia

Silvia is an eleven-year-old girl, in therapy at three sessions per week. For about a year, she has been suffering from severe panic attacks. She has trouble going to school, playing sports, and leaving the house. She lost her mother aged seven, and about a year ago one of her mother's old friends, whom her father has started seeing, moved in with them.

In our first few sessions, Silvia is rather unwilling to talk to me, insisting that this take place in the presence of the woman who has taken her mother's place. Generally speaking, such a period of hesitation signals a traumatic precedent of such significance that it renders the subject deeply wary of any sort of new experience. Silvia's disappointment is defined by a real sense of grief, and her father's coupling with her mother's friend forcefully brings the trauma back.

After an initial period of resistance, Silvia eventually agrees to see me alone, pouring out an enormous amount of affection into the analytic situation and placing upon it a great deal of expectations. With my help, she seems able to rebuild the condition of prematurely lost illusion; it is as if the analytic bond has conjured a feeling that disappeared abruptly with her mother's death, and Silvia seeks to replace the unbridgeable emptiness that ensued. She brings me her favourite games, tacitly requesting that I allow her to win, and speaks to me insistently of her desire to have a pet dog. Though she has a sister who is two years younger, she feels lonely when nobody pays her any attention. Her father's probable denial of mourning—which deprived Silvia of the opportunity to share her pain in a loving relationship—has made her loneliness very evident, and aggravated her condition as a little girl so sorely tried by life's events.

At times, in the transference, Silvia experiences me as the mother who is still alive, or as the replacement object with which to share the lack of the mother. One day, she brings a dream in which she goes up into the sky to visit her mother. Sometimes, in the countertransference, I experience her as a daughter who has fallen from the heavens. At the end of our sessions, Silvia says goodbye—almost as if to preserve "the sense of continuity of [her] existence" (Winnicott, 2001b[1949], p. 189; see also Mascagni's reading, 1995)—by kissing me on the cheek and reminding me of the date of our next session. These two signals appear to concretise the sense that our relationship is a place for the restoration of illusion and, therefore, a place of potential working through.

A few months into the therapy, I suggest that Silvia draw some pictures, and she finds much enjoyment in these doodles—a game, as Pontalis (1988, p. 184, translated for this edition) writes, "to look together for what we don't know . . . an understanding of the circulation of signifiers between two subjects". In her doodles, a cuddly toy repeatedly appears—her favourite, she tells me, when she was a little girl. She says she would like to bring in and show me this cuddly toy, which is half dog, half bear and wears a bib on which "Hug me" is written. She recalls asking her father what the words meant. From our next meeting, "Huggy" becomes an attentive spectator of our sessions, an intermediary for our emotions. At the beginning of sessions, Silvia asks me to hold Huggy to warm him up; she then places him on the table between us, and talks to me about Huggy, or to Huggy about herself. Facilitated by what is clearly a transitional object recovered from her early childhood, Silvia can communicate her past history and daily sorrows. Through the transference, she can relive the illusion of creating the object, while being able to detach herself from it, seeing as it can be created anew.

Dialogue becomes easier after this. Silvia tells me about herself, speaking to me directly. Huggy is consulted only when feelings become very strong and she asks for his help remembering. The idea of bringing Huggy to the sessions renders the analytic situation more contained and fluid, rich in narrative events which also include me, turning me into a character in Silvia's story. Huggy becomes a centre of thought, an *elsewhere* providing dynamism and allowing us to escape a duality that might be excessively confusing or exciting. At times, Silvia uses Huggy to suggest things about herself for me to interpret—"Didn't Huggy tell you that I felt lonely this weekend?"— or to reproach my misunderstandings: "Huggy didn't explain this properly. I didn't want to go out on my own, not because I'm afraid of growing up, but because I could tell that my dad didn't want me to." Like her parents, I would ask Silvia to be grown up or child-like according to my therapeutic expectations, and this was her way of inviting me to act with more tact and insight.

As her trust gradually grows, Silvia speaks of her difficult relationship with her sister—a relationship that bespeaks a difficult attempt to control a traumatic rupture of a narcissistic context. Silvia reveals feelings of anxiety, telling me about when, as a small child, she would assert her dominance by tying her sister to a chair and frighten her by pushing it over. Her mother, who was still alive back then but sick with cancer, disapproved of such violent games and would ask Silvia to behave responsibly and maturely. The mother's lengthy illness had perhaps inhibited the rivalry and competition between siblings, and had led Silvia to experience a part of herself through her sister. In this omnipotent construction, Silvia protected her mother from her sister's aggression by identifying with the mother. Her mother's death threw this omnipotent mechanism into crisis, and made Silvia aware of her need to reappropriate her aggression—not least the probable unconscious fantasy of having contributed to her mother's death, burdened further by incestuous fantasies involving her father. After her mother's death, Silvia was suddenly forced to become a mother without being one.

When the tone of our sessions is lighter, Silvia tells me stories about her sister, playing the role of a mother who is concerned about her daughter; on a less conscious level, with the recovery of Huggy the cuddly toy as a transitional object, she articulates her difficulty reconciling her dependence and aggression in relating to her classmates.

When her sister falls briefly ill, Silvia's anxieties return. During the session in which she talks about this sickness, I do not verbally interpret her anxiety as aggression, and the next time we are scheduled to meet, Silvia's father calls to say she is not feeling well and will not be coming. My not offering a swift interpretation, perhaps, has contributed to Silvia's falling ill, has provoked her into revealing herself for the first time.

In the session following her illness, Silvia brings more explicit material that bespeaks her contrasting feelings. Ambivalence leads to disenchantment: she becomes less controlling of her sister, finding the courage to face external reality despite its unpredictability. It is at this time—approximately two years from the beginning of the therapy—that Silvia begins to menstruate, and with this change come a host of adolescent issues linked to friendships and love.

At this point, we face a matter of analytic technique, concerning the dynamics of the relationship. Here, the therapist adopts a disposition that supports illusion, and it is clear how important this is for Silvia. Winnicott (2005a, p. 15) writes,

> The mother, at the beginning, by an almost 100 per cent adaptation affords the infant the opportunity for the *illusion* that her breast is part of the infant. It is, as it were, under magical control . . . Omnipotence is nearly a fact of experience. The mother's eventual task is gradually to disillusion the infant, but she has no hope of success unless at first she has been able to give sufficient opportunity for illusion.

How, though, might we tell when there has been sufficient "opportunity for illusion" to begin to disillusion, but not disappoint? And how to be sure not to run the risk that, by prolonging the illusion, the omnipotent mechanism could, on contact with external reality, fail once again and cause disappointment? Should the therapist here, for example, have interpreted Silvia's anxiety for her sister's passing illness as determined by her fear of recognising her aggression as her own? And if so, when?

In the analytic relationship, the decision on how and when to prolong or end illusion does not depend on the analyst's technical competence, but on the coming together of her personal history of illusion, disillusion, and disappointment with the patient's transference history—an encounter, defined by compatibility and incompatibility, between the analyst's moment of identity and the patient's. It is, moreover, possible to work through the illusion–disillusionment relationship as it progresses and observe its uses *a posteriori*. One cannot, however, derive from it a technique *a priori*, pertaining, as it does, to the more primitive and unconscious emotional levels of the therapist's relationship with the patient. The possibility of engendering a sense of illusion, combined with trust, is located in a profound satisfactory experience, unthreatened by unpredictable disappointment and strengthened by the capacity to bear disillusionment, thus allowing the therapist to avoid being overwhelmed by destructive unconscious phantasies. It is not useful, however, to support the experience of omnipotence when, in the face of the threat of a real separation, the therapist continues to see the relationship as idyllic and untouchable. In this way, the therapist—while supporting the potential for illusion—is, at the same time, aware of the emergence of the patient's need to separate, and able to acknowledge it, without eluding the unconscious drives in all developmental directions. Since the ability to sustain illusion in the other overlaps with the other's propensity for illusion, this creates the possibility that the two potential areas contribute to the construction of a shared space, where it is possible to separate while remaining in a continuous relationship, as aspects of union and separation in the relationship oscillate.

Such open-endedness also makes it difficult for the therapist to escape from illusion and find the right moment in which the patient can tolerate interpretation breaking it. It seems to me that what happens most frequently—in both the mother–child and patient–analyst pairing—is that external reality breaks into the relational situation, altering it forever. In reality, the mother cannot be perennially present, and frees herself from the child as she frees the child of herself, thus helping the child grow; in the same way, the analyst breaks the illusion that has been created by using her and the patient's reality. In such cases, the child tends to revert to play, in which he can take possession of a space of illusion–disillusion. This continues as the child grows up, either remaining as play or being articulated as creativity and artistic expression.

The Winnicottian model is, fundamentally, a relational one, in the sense that it is based on the primary need of a good experience that permits the subject to stray from it without consequentially losing it. For Freud, lack arises as the original trauma, which sets in motion thought's creative and compensatory activity (the "fort–da" game), and emancipates the individual from perceptual sensoriality (Masciangelo, 1988). For Winnicott, the sensory and perceptive continuity of the shared space of illusion allows the dilemma of recognition–denial of absence to be dispersed and diluted. Freud identifies the limits of illusion and encourages, instead, the stoical acceptance of pain, coming to the melancholy conclusion that "To tolerate life remains, after all, the first duty of all living beings. Illusion becomes valueless if it makes this harder for us" (1915b, p. 298). For Winnicott, illusion is not imbued with this melancholy and, when the infant begins to play, he sees the human need for illusion as an ontological foundation of the subject (Kluzer Usuelli, 1992).

Creativity of thought is a product of the long process of working through transitional phenomena. The possibility of communication through the written word is also a form of illusion, a capacity to create and perpetuate illusion for the self and others. This is why, despite the inherent fragility and tenuousness of what is produced, we cannot suppress our desire to continue to communicate. In fact, illusion is so strong that, when profoundly shared, it transcends and goes beyond the individual. This recalls Italian poet Ugo Foscolo's observations on death and mourning, in these moving lines from his poem *Dei Sepolcri* [The Sepulchers]:

> But why should man before his time
> Be deprived of the illusion that even in death
> He may linger on the threshold of Hell?
> Does he not live on, below the loam,
> Unhearing of the harmony of day,

If he awakens this illusion in the minds
Of loved ones who tend his grave? Divine
Is this communion with the cherished dead,
A gift from heaven to men.

> (1808, p. 8, translated for this edition)

Illusion certainly offers comfort to the ego; it allows us to defer death, either as an extension beyond life, or as a capacity to divert the death drive activated by disillusion (i.e., the recognition of lack). If the ego's function is its ability to correspond to the self, to what we call our identity, illusion (which is also an illusion of self-sufficiency and omnipotence) temporally supports the ego while it works on acquiring this ability in reality rather than illusion. The essential outline of this path is traced in the earliest experiences with an object capable of both illusion and disillusion, to such a variable degree that every life experience is a singular one and identity, in turn, is always an unpredictable destination.

CHAPTER THREE

Identity: internal objects and the superego

I nternal objects are precipitates in the ego of the experience of an object. They represent relationships with external objects, modi-fied by drives and fantasies, which can either be transformed by their development or remain primitively fixed and impossible to work through, causing conflict and suffering. It is my contention, through clinical experiences with child therapies, that in the latter case we should speak of precipitates in the superego rather than the ego, and that it is analytic therapy that tends to transform this indigestible, conflictual core into more collaborative contents for the ego.

Klein (1927) argues that the superego does not coincide with the introjection of the parents; indeed, one can encounter very gentle parents of children with a very severe superego. Freud goes so far as to compare this agency to a non-personified force of destiny: "The last figure in the series that began with the parents is the dark power of Destiny which only the fewest of us are able to look upon as imper-sonal" (1924, p. 168). Some years later, he goes on to argue,

A child's super-ego is in fact constructed on the model not of its parents but of its parents' super-ego; the contents which fill it are the same and it becomes the vehicle of tradition and of all the time-resisting judgements of value which have propagated themselves in this manner from generation to generation. (1933a, p. 67)

The phenomena I wish to describe are observed mainly in children who have not had sufficient experience of illusion in the Winnicottian sense. Instead of introjecting objects that become the ego, in these pathological conditions it seems to me that a thickening of the super-ego or a splitting in the body occurs, as a compromise between appropriation and keeping separate from the self. The superego would, thus, function as a boundary zone at the meeting point between the ego and the outside world—an agency that, in one sense, belongs to the ego, and, in another sense, remains foreign to it.

In *The Ego and the Id* (1923b), Freud speaks of the formation of the superego as a form of ego ideal, a place where experiences that are, so to speak, better or higher may continue to exist. But when, in clinical work, we encounter a cruel superego that is much more reminiscent of a delinquent urge, can we still trace it back to a higher ethical instance? And would this be ethical in the way that an executioner might punish any slight mistake or shortcoming? This superego could well emblematise the so-called carer who shows scant consideration for the child's condition, making excessive requests, expecting the child to be infallible; or perhaps even a transgenerational superegoic content, handed down compulsively from parent to child in all its cruelty.

The superego could, I think, be seen as a sort of limbo in which identifications of strongly ambivalent objects are kept suspended, forbidden to the ego by the objects themselves, even before any triangulation can occur. In this case, it might be useful to read the theory of the ego–superego alongside theories of the internal object and transitional area.

Internal objects have no definable borders, are with the ego but also distinguished from it. To see the internal object as a superegoic component would mean that the object cannot be introjected entirely, but is instead kept suspended, available both for introjection and projection. This pertains, of course, to objects that have strong persecutory qualities—either because they bear the subject's anger or because they have invested the subject exclusively with expulsive needs. It would take a transformation of this (prevalently schizo-paranoid) condition to lead to a more peaceful integration of these objects.

In Chapter Five, I consider the difficulty of integrating the introjection of our experiences of objects, and how, in such cases, one possibility for keeping them at a distance is to relegate them to the body. (On the subject, see Hinshelwood (1994) on hypochondria.) I will not focus here solely on this aspect, but also consider the problems caused when objects are "imprisoned" (Klein, 2017[1940]) not only in the body but in the psychic area Freud called the superego, as distinguished from the ego. I believe that the superegoic component of identity is fundamental to the psychic adjustment between life and death drives, satisfaction and destruction. Any excess of this component—whether persecutory and omnipresent, or absent and oblivious to all sense of boundaries—engenders suffering and pathology.

Roberto

At the time of consultation, Roberto is ten years old. His parents bring him to me because he overeats and suffers from being teased at school for his chubbiness, which has not yet developed into full-blown obesity. The family dynamics are complex: Roberto's father drinks and Roberto's mother, who is perpetually on a diet, is particularly distressed by Roberto's weight. Both his parents fear that their son's greed and consequential bodyweight might degenerate.

His family background immediately leads me to suspect that Roberto is the chosen recipient of an imposing and destructive orality. Roberto is very jealous of his five-year-old brother, who embodies, in both appearance and behaviour, the nice and good part desired by his parents. This hypothesis of a double mandate makes the difficulty of appeasing the conflict between the two brothers easier to understand; indeed, Roberto expresses a great deal of anger about the way his parents treat his brother as if he were infallible.

Speaking of the differences between the two children, Roberto's mother tells me that she had difficulty breastfeeding Roberto and getting him to fall asleep. She blames her inexperience and her eldest son's anxiety; with the second, she says, she felt more adequate. Whatever the reasons, neither Roberto nor his mother were able to have the illusion of being "the other", or "being for the other". As Klein argues,

> Unpleasant experiences and the lack of enjoyable ones, in the young child, especially lack of happy and close contact with loved people, increase ambivalence, diminish trust and hope and confirm anxieties about inner annihilation and external persecution. (2017[1940], p. 347).

Another reason why Roberto is brought to therapy is his restless behaviour at school. His grades, especially in mathematics, are not good, though he shows a great passion for history and says he would like to be an archaeologist someday, thereby demonstrating a certain capacity to sublimate.

From the very beginning of our twice-weekly sessions, Roberto wants to play a war game. The game, which is very repetitive, unfolds loosely like this: first, Roberto distributes toy soldiers, bombs, and weaponry on the battlefield, reserving the most powerful for himself; his attacks then wreak great destruction on the rival forces, which are left almost impotent; finally, to keep the game from ending too quickly, he elects some enemy heroes to put up one last struggle before being definitively defeated. During these military manoeuvres, Roberto is visibly exhilarated, getting carried away with shouts representing gunfire and explosions, in which his whole body seems to take part.

The game reveals Roberto's need to triumph over his brother and, through this military struggle, also over his parents' designs—to find his own way of asserting himself, rather than to pursue a maniacal form of possession. In real life, Roberto is unable to fulfil his desire for self-assertion, because it is closely linked with the idea that destroying the other is tantamount to also destroying the parts of the self that are projected in the other. In our sessions, however, he is very happy to play this war game: it is as if he can make use of its brutality to conceive of the possibility of implementing the aggression of his instincts and internal objects, while also being able to witness that both survive the process. Not only is Roberto's aggression present throughout the game, I also have the impression there is strong sexual arousal.

As the therapy continues, Roberto finds his progress satisfying. Some months later, in fact, when monthly payment is due, he asks me how much the sessions cost. "That's a lot but I need it" is his answer to my reply. Further confirmation comes with the variations in Roberto's war game, which becomes less violent as it progresses. The child remains calmer, and as he distributes the soldiers and bombs more equitably, he talks to me about having a hard time at school, where a classmate has been calling him an "ugly fatty".

Roberto turns to his father for advice, asking him what he had done when he was at school and classmates had made fun of him. His father tells him stories of his countless acts of bravery, encouraging Roberto to defend himself with his fists just like he used to. Roberto's father's attitude seems entirely detached from his son's reality, and even the young boy appears dismayed by it. I try to suggest that perhaps Roberto's father already sees him as a strong and courageous young man, while he still feels like a child who needs to be defended. It becomes increasingly possible to distinguish the child of our early sessions—who always wanted to play and win his war game, as if due to a parental mandate—from the child at the mercy of his instincts who appears frightened and ashamed and asks pragmatically for help.

Roberto talks repeatedly about his schoolmates' tendency to gang up on him. He complains about what goes on but also speaks of its importance somewhat hyperbolically, perhaps because this allows him to locate, outside of the home environment, a superegoic adjustment that is already familiar to him. Roberto's parents often rebuke him for not being more self-controlled and responsible—that is, not exercising the superegoic function they themselves require so much, which they have not been able to provide him with, but have asked of him insistently. Consequently, the sole superegoic agency that Roberto can use is punitive and not regulative, and devalues and depresses him, without providing a containment function.

Children who have experienced illusion, in the Winnicottian sense of "being the object" (2005a), have experienced an object created solely for them, with which they can identify and from which they can separate without trauma. Instead, children who have experienced a disappointing object—in a fundamental conflict keeping the relationship in the state of developmental impossibility—are led to perpetuate this impasse. In the experience of illusion, affirmation of the self is continuous and never destructive. The use of the object, as Winnicott intends it, means destroying the object, having the courage and confidence to be able to do so without fear of losing it forever. When the object can be created, the ego identifies with the object created; if there is no illusion, the qualities of the object cannot be integrated, remain foreign, and possess more of a superegoic than an egoic nature.

To one session, Roberto brings the board game Monopoly® and announces that he wants to challenge me. What strikes me is not so much the challenge (we had, after all, come from a long experience of war games), but rather the increase in his self-confidence: for the first time, he is able to share a set of external rules without feeling crushed. Moreover, Monopoly® is a game he knows very well, which, therefore, he manages to win—not by magic, but by applying strategy and skill. At the end, Roberto shows he is also capable of a reparative attitude toward me, attributing part of his victory to good luck.

The change from the insatiable, chaotic destructiveness of war to the need for order and control over things indicates that the expulsive need begins to give way to the anal capacity to retain. This also suggests that there are internal movements towards the integration of the ego and its objects, which is expressed by the subject's greater confidence in having an internal space, and being able to occupy a definite space in the world. The sense of loss of the object is less persecutory and not ineluctable.

After our long and hard-fought game of Monopoly®, Roberto invents a new game, an adaptation of his war game. He decides that the two opposing forts have become two bases for territorial exploration, and that the soldiers are, in fact, archaeologists exploring the subsoil in search of a buried civilisation. As we play, Roberto says he feels happy. I get the impression that he has gone in search of his internal objects, found parts of them, and repositioned them in a beneficial way.

Two years pass and, in the sessions before the summer holidays, Roberto is very worried that, given his improvements, his parents will not bring him back to therapy after the break. In fact, it is precisely because Roberto recognises the bond with his therapist that he also feels the desire to no longer depend on it. His projection of this onto his parents seems a way to distance the conflict, but also potentially mediate the projected aspect.

Tellingly, Roberto succeeds in convincing his parents to let him resume therapy after the summer holidays. The possibility of spending another year in therapy allows Roberto to begin to talk about, rather than enacting, his relationships with his parents, brother, and schoolmates, showing a developed use of language and communication, which proves he has passed from latency to a more properly pubertal stage.

Lucia

Lucia is a seven-year-old girl, whose parents bring for consultation as a result of school difficulties and a tendency to isolate herself from her schoolmates. She has an elder brother of eighteen, and, before she was born, her parents lost a son at the age of six for unknown causes. Stricken by their son's death, Lucia's parents tried repeatedly to have another child, and Lucia was born precisely from this impossibility of grieving. In fact, Lucia's mother (who is in therapy herself) realises that she raised the little girl with the nagging anxiety that she would lose her, beleaguering the child with prohibitions and orders. When discussing Lucia's infancy with me, she says she was bottle-fed and was always unwilling to eat.

In the early stages of her tri-weekly therapy, Lucia varies between two games. In one, set in a classroom, she is the teacher with the whiteboard and I am her pupil; in the other, set in a restaurant, she is the pushy, overbearing waiter and I am the customer. The teacher is strict and short-tempered—she starts writing maths problems on the board but never finishes them, anxiously trying to do too many things at once. Lucia is transferring the frustrations of her school life onto me; when I suggest this to her, there is a small attenuation of her sternness and anxiety.

In cases like these, I often find that the first thing children who have a difficult or impossible relationship with their internal objects seek to do in analysis is attend to these internal objects. It is as if children know that without an adequate object there can be no vital experience of the self. The self presents itself in analysis as a suspended experience, which remains fundamentally undecided as to whether it will pursue life or death; this involves the construction of an adequate object—not in the sense that the therapist taking the mother's place solves the problem, but, rather, that the therapist is willing to collect the patient's painful projections so that she can process and transform them and, thus, build an adequate object.

In Lucia's games, the despotic teacher or force-feeding waiter represent an archaic superego that stands in place of the object, like an unfeeling, hardened mechanism, and this is Lucia's only way of relating to others. She had been anxiously conceived in the wake of her brother's death, to fill a void of disorientation and pain, but was then left to grow up without her parents paying much attention to her needs. It was only when she started having academic problems that her parents began to realise their little girl was suffering, sucking her fingers, picking away at her skin, masturbating while watching television, and displaying a strong tendency for dramatisations that verged on delusion. Her brother, who died so mysteriously, hovers like an ever-present ghost occupying the mind of her parents and, consequently, Lucia's.

As therapy progresses, Lucia increasingly reveals the severity of her symptoms and her way of establishing contact with objects. It seems that she does not employ a psychic mode, regressively establishing an exclusively bodily contact instead, in a way she imitates from her family environment or the television: kissing on the mouth, touching, pretend copulation, masturbation. The intensity of these displays preoccupies me a great deal. While I allow her to represent lovers getting married and embracing one another—in itself, a way to portray the need for contact with the psychic and symbolic—I shrink from her more concrete demands of eroticism by trying to interpret how her infantile need is deformed by images of adults who do not recognise a child's need for tenderness. I am reminded of Ferenczi's essay "The confusion of tongues: the language of passion and the language of tenderness" (1932), and Laplanche's reading of it in the context of the theory of generalised seduction by way of Freud's theory of drives (Laplanche, 1989; Algini & De Silvestris, 1992).

After approximately two years of therapy, Lucia brings a doll to the session, which comes to represent the little girl she "has given birth to with great effort", and which she diligently feeds by bottle. She and I are the parents that look after her lovingly. It appears that, through the doll, Lucia can begin to construct an object for herself. The need to preserve is so strong that, at the end of each session, she asks me to remember the games we have played for next time. Lucia is now sure she is being listened to—she is now also able to speak of the tortured body, rather than just the excited or maniacally exhibited one.

Lucia represents Peter Pan fighting Captain Hook to save the lost boys and give them shelter, to acknowledge the part of her that is suffering and its need for treatment. To take care of the most painful aspect of her self, she transfers it to me. Her favourite game becomes playing the mother who tells me off for picking at the skin around my nails until it bleeds. When she arrives at our sessions, she checks my hands and threatens to take me to hospital and have them cut off if she finds any of my cuticles raised. Lucia stages the anxiety of her parents, who experience their daughter in a persecutory manner. By investing her with their projections, to distance themselves from her suffering, they repress and stifle her.

My repeated meetings with Lucia's parents prove very useful, and their collaboration is indispensable. Lucia's school difficulties—clearly linked to an ego so engaged with her internal situation that it cannot deal with the outside world—make it necessary for a tutor to be called in to help her regularly with her homework. Lucia's confidence increases; in therapy, she uses the school game to express her ability to work on the fragmented objects that make her suffer. She casts herself as the teacher of unreliable and dangerous children; I am her assistant and do everything in my power to help her with her difficult task. The psychic confidence that Lucia gradually builds up—both with the psychological work and with the care she puts into her schoolwork—leads her to be more cohesive, and, thus, to cope better with her excitement and aggression. After six years of analysis, she shows me that she has stopped picking at her hands with her teeth and informs me that her academic progress is such that she has finished her first year of secondary school with good grades.

In the two cases described, the parent–child relationship is particularly superegoic in nature, and the children respond by relegating an indigestible parental core to the body. This perverse relationship reproaches the child's inability to function, while, at the same time, contributing heavily to this inability. The parental core is so indigestible that, more often than not, it is dragged from generation to generation. In both cases, the parents have difficult histories, in which they have had to manage a considerable amount of acted out and life-threatening aggression. Roberto's parents have a history of deprivation, bereavement, and alcoholism; Lucia's parents have experienced periods of extreme difficulty and rebellion. Roberto and Lucia consequently carry the baggage of an atavistic conflict that still needs to be worked through (Faimberg, 2005), and are so absorbed by it that little space for the ego remains. This explains their difficulties in having internal relations with objects that are distant in time, and also with the outside world, which is similarly unrecognisable. Roberto clashes in both fantasy and reality with a living brother; Lucia is continuously in the grip of a dead body—the ghost of her brother constantly evoked in the pain of her parents' interminable mourning, which is more conducive to delusional thought than working through.

The cases of these two children show us how the working through of primary identifications is fundamental for the possibility of opening up to the oedipal experience. The experience foregrounds the importance of being a subject, just as it is then necessary to find a personal solution to the oedipal event for the formation and constitution of identity.

CHAPTER FOUR

Identity: from oedipal vicissitudes to adolescence

I believe that any attempt to insert so-called oedipal constellations into established theoretical frames is invariably reductionist. There are innumerable oedipal vicissitudes, just as there are innumerable individuals, each with their own specificities. I shall, therefore, identify some particular developmental lines, based on my clinical experience and my own perspective, making no claim to generalisation. Evidently, more often than not, we find ourselves observing clinically pathological predicaments of subjects whose development has gone awry, marked by a disjunction between biological and psychical development. I have the impression, for instance, that children and adolescents who come into therapy all suffer from a developmental delay, which implies, at the very least, that they have not resolved their Oedipus complex. This lack of resolution appears all the more dramatic in as much as the Oedipus complex (as representative of a traumatic and conflictual situation) is an essential part of childhood amnesia—whether by disavowal, splitting, or repression.

Consequently, and accordingly, the phase of latency paves the way to the adolescent configuration, as mainly psychotic or neurotic. In a sense, latency could be thought of as a time of working through which, recapitulating infantile experiences, reaches the point where it is possible to articulate these experiences within a whole self and a whole object that can integrate them. Alternatively, the presentation of the divisions and projections that traverse the self and the object can prevail, striving at least for a compromise solution between that which can be tolerated and acknowledged as belonging to the ego and that which cannot be tolerated or integrated. This dichotomy, however, is a radicalisation produced by our theory making and perhaps does not exist in nature. Both modes of latency functioning, thus defined, coexist in variable portions, whether the oedipal constellation evolves towards a more or less healthy resolution (as Winnicott defines the psychoneurotic solution) or whether the result is a "psychotic necessity" (where necessity indicates an extreme defence of the ego).

If latency is to be seen as the phase that follows the waning of the Oedipus complex, it is very much influenced by how the child goes through this waning—or, as Ferrari argues in *From the Eclipse of the Body to the Dawn of Thought* (2004), the oedipal constellation never wanes completely. On the subject of latency, in the *Three Essays on the Theory of Sexuality* (1905d), Freud speaks of the construction of "mental forces which are later to impede the course of the sexual instinct and, like dams, restrict its flow—disgust, feelings of shame, and the claims of aesthetic and moral ideals" (1905d, p. 177). Although the child's upbringing contributes strongly to the construction of these dams, Freud continues, this development is organically determined, is hereditary, and would come about even without the contribution of the child's educators. These constructions, which are so important for the individual's subsequent civilisation and normality, are set in place at the expense of the child's sexual drives, which do not cease to be active all throughout the latency period, but their drive energy is deviated from their sexual discharge towards different aims.

Latency puts all the defences available to the ego to the test. The therapist, Winnicott maintains, must take into account the fact that the barely integrated ego feels easily threatened and that, when it is engaged in making a synthesis of its own experiences, it is difficult for the ego to deal with the analysis or to think that something might be wrong and commit to the treatment. For the same reason, latency children are unlikely to get into analysis willingly, unless they have unconsciously succeeded in developing a symptom that their parents find alarming, because they are reminded of similar aspects they struggled with in their own oedipal situation and its difficult resolution.

In *Le jeu en psychothérapie de l'enfant* [Playing in Child Psychotherapy] (2000), Anzieu and colleagues describe latency as a "position", in the meaning that Klein gives to the term. "Autoerotism that replaces the manifestations of the oedipal drive", Anzieu writes,

> is a characteristic of that which I prefer to call *latency position*. The changes that children go through between four and twelve years of age which, in our times, are very different from those prevailing at the time when Freud discovered infantile sexuality, are very apparent and influence the image that adults have of them. Latency means that something is in a state of suspension. It could be sexual development or its later reworking in the course of the life cycle. It could also be the depressive movement that such reworking inevitably elicits and the renunciations it entails (Anzieu et al., 2000, p. 91, translated for this edition)

Marco is ten years old and has a sister aged seven. His parents do not pay much attention to him. He is brought in for therapy because he is unable to fall asleep if his parents go out at night. This has been the case for the past two years. The triggering element occurred when his parents sent him—aged eight, and with his consent—on holiday for a month with his friend and their family. They had had to go and collect him in tears a few days later. Since then, Marco does not want to spend the night away from home, even at his grandparents' place, where he often used to sleep when he was little.

All this irritates Marco's parents a great deal, especially his mother. Evidently, when Marco attempted to go without his parents aged eight, he genuinely believed he had sufficiently disposed of the bond with them; instead, distance had revealed a lack of identification with his own objects, which, experienced as an intolerable lack, had produced the anxiety that had made him backpedal. All this, therefore, led me to believe that Marco had come to me in a regressive condition, asking to be accompanied in latency (i.e., in the working through of the oedipal relationship). In relation to this, I will discuss two stories Marco came up with, within a short interval of time, in our sessions. These narratives, with their imaginary, magical quality, have the quality of conscious psychic productions, because they reveal and, at the same time, conceal deeper contents such as play and dreams.

In the first story Marco tells me (which I will summarise briefly), two friends have to climb a mountain. They encounter several dangers—represented by a woman and a cruel cat—but are helped by a man, who lends them a good little animal as a pet. The pet urges the two friends to avoid the "tricks" of the dangerous woman and her cat, so the two decide to avoid the whole undertaking and turn back.

If we take into account that Marco's story comes at a time when it seems, especially through some of his drawings, that he is trying to grapple with masculine identity, climbing the mountain (an image that has also appeared before) could be understood as the capacity for erection, a rising up over childhood. The story could be seen as an expression of his doubts about putting himself to the test. Indeed, he has clearly chosen to regress and rely instead upon an infantile aspect, represented by the good pet (pregenital sexuality), which permits the avoidance of genital seduction (the "tricks" of the woman and her cat). This situation is facilitated by the transference activating a regression, not only as the child's defence against separation (appearance of desire = separation), but perhaps also because, within the analytic relationship, he experiences the analyst as an object that avoids recognising sexual investment, thus amplifying the fear of such an investment. And if we relate this to the fact that Marco's mother clearly tended to repress his development, treating him like a needy little boy, we can assume that another type of conflict might be in play. Essentially, Marco represented himself as the phallus of the mother, gratified by the fact that this was the only way his mother afforded him any dignity, as if to say: you are male only if you are mine.

Marco thus finds himself embroiled in a conflict. If he separates from his mother, this separation could only mean castration for both him and his mother; if he does not, he is compelled to renounce the need to affirm his own identity. Furthermore, both he and his mother would be accomplices in such a defensive solution, representing their union as omnipotent and self-sufficient, to protect themselves from incest (i.e., from the sexual desire that arises after separation and individuation). Marco would not climb the mountain to avoid the separation that would have led to the appearance of desire and seduction, an experience culminating in incest. From his point of view, perhaps, he could find no economical reason to pursue this separation, which alluded to the prospect of adolescence. Marco's story very clearly represents his condition of latency, the psychic state in which one senses transformational drives together with their inhibition. Anzieu and colleagues write,

It is possible to understand latency as a moment of pause which links up to important psychic movements at the service of libido. When these processes cannot be disengaged from archaic or pregenital positions, whether for internal or external reasons, the ego regresses and re-finds depressive states from which it can only break free in pathological ways. The symptom is often a compromise solution of the conflict with the superego. Inhibition is a typical example: external needs enter into conflict and the ego defends itself with regression. The symptom shows which part of the internal world is the place of conflict, or which choice the ego has been able to make to express its weakness ... The symptom is enlisted to express infantile helplessness. This waiting can be called "latency" and can be reproduced throughout life, when events cause a depressive process and the need to make important psychic readjustments, such as, for example, mourning ... Psychotherapy in latency, therefore, consists in the search for new ways to overcome a crisis linked to oedipal conflict and facilitate the entry into adolescence. It is a period of mourning and maturation. (Anzieu et al., 2000, p. 94–95, translated for this edition)

Working with children of this age has reinforced my conviction that latency is a state of the ego in relation to reality, and is a process that relates to both instinctual and superegoic internal events. It is a psychic state because it is structural, and is a process because it has a genesis and a development. These two aspects intersect and intertwine continuously, promoting the child's ability to take an interest in others in the extent to which he can preserve himself.

Shortly after the first story, Marco comes up with another, in response to an interpretation I suggest regarding the cartoon characters he draws, which are always deprived of a nose. I relate this absence to a defence from the perception of painful and unpleasant experiences. Told in the style of a fairytale, Marco's story is about a boy who wakes up one morning without a nose. Instead of going to school, he decides to run away from home. Many days pass, and the boy begins to feel remorse for what he has done. At this point in the story, a goblin shows up and returns his nose, provided that he promises to appreciate it.

The story makes me think of Gogol's "The Nose", a short story about Collegiate Assessor Major Kovalyov, who loses and then regains his nose as if by a miracle. Marco's story puts us both in a good mood, as it seems to reflect aspects of the analytic development. By suddenly recalling Gogol's tale, I could also establish an internal continuity between past and present, which could, in turn, be related to Marco's outlook like a kind of equivalence: just as I remember my past, you will be able to remember your present.

Marco stripped of his nose is, perhaps, a representation of himself deprived of his sexuality, to prevent his desires from encountering insurmountable obstacles—such as incest—or the terrible guilt of hatred, or an image of the mother as separate from him. It was a representation of self-mutilation, as if to eliminate anything that could have created conflict between the self and reality in the process of growing up and becoming independent. Only remorse for this abdication from himself could permit him to regain possession of his nose, and, thus, maintain self-regard even in the face of these conflictual aspects. With his story, Marco perhaps also wanted to make me aware of his desire to be appreciated in the expression of his sexual identity—an identity that, with the appearance of the goblin, he was contemplating as a possibility.

Marco continues to bring stories of this nature—narratives that, I think, bespeak a continuous oscillation between a tentative figuration of his entry into adolescence, and a simultaneous withdrawal from, and subsequent return to, it. I feel able to tolerate these hesitations, and, therefore, refrain from pushing for progress or being excessively disappointed by regression. I believe that the working through and construction of a more developed mode of functioning must be grounded on the fact that the previous modes can be preserved.

In the transition from latency to adolescence, we witness, in our clinical practice, a continuous toing and froing between an infantile search for parental support and attempts to embrace independence. In these cases, profound core identity is constituted by a continuously developing body image, in the sense that psychic transformations are sparked by the body's transformations as puberty progresses.

CHAPTER FIVE

The laborious integration of the body image in adolescence

A dolescents who seek analysis face the difficulties of negotiating adolescent turmoil and the shaking up of the provisional identity of the infantile defences, alongside a sense of openness to new potentials. These potentials are the changes the adolescent has to face, along with establishing self-boundaries and making choices.

Adolescence is like a state of illness that is both temporary and normal. In his play *Spring Awakening*, Frank Wedekind stages the dramatic nature of this period of transition, focusing on the discovery of the body and sexuality, which he sees occurring "the way a frightened owl flies through a burning forest" (2007[1891], p. 34). In a letter of 1891, in which he discusses the play with a critic, Wedekind speaks of his intention to provide a poetic representation of the onset of puberty in adolescence, in the hope of contributing to our comprehension of the phenomenon. Little did he know how much he succeeded in shedding light on the topic! His farsighted intuitions prefigure the most recent theories proposed by psychoanalysts who treat adolescents—theories that focus on the importance of the integration of the body image of the self as a man or woman.

It is useful, before we proceed, to distinguish between the concepts of adolescence and the adolescent. The former concerns a phase in life which it is impossible not to encounter, while the ensuing process—and the ways of avoiding, resisting or traversing it—is always a particular and unique constellation that a specific adolescent devises in the throes of puberty. In her book *New Maladies of the Soul* (1995), Kristeva does not give adolescence a temporal framework, regarding it, instead, as an open psychic structure to which the analyst must continue to listen. For Kristeva, adolescence is like a metaphor of that which is still unformed, a mirage of the prelinguistic realm and the undecided body.

Adolescents find themselves in a paradoxical situation. In order to find their bearings in the world, they need to be firmly rooted to their origins; at the same time, however, they need to differentiate themselves from these origins, and be free to distance themselves from them. It is, therefore, conceivable that adolescents almost always find themselves having to actualise this paradox through a series of split identifications. The ego—as the psychic agency prevalently facing outwards to reality—needs to free itself from its functions of mediation and preservation of family ties, and, thus, be free not to identify with the objects it is detaching from. It is precisely at this time that the body, in as much as it is body ego, can become a great resource as an auxiliary ego that gathers together the identifications with the lost objects. These "identification conversions", as Deutsch calls them (1959), are successful from an economical point of view—in unburdening the ego—when splitting mechanisms manage to relegate them in bodily aspects whose origin the ego does not easily and quickly recognise. Examples of this might be, for instance, slow chronic metabolic disorders, alterations of the organic automatic nervous system, motor automatisms, and the gestures and postures that are reminiscent of significant experiences in the parent–child relationship and are, thus, condensed in a bodily *gestalt*.

Deutsch discusses "identification conversions" in his book *On the Mysterious Leap from the Mind to the Body* (1959), in which he addresses symbolisations, body identifications, and conversions, building on an attentive reading of Freud's conception of the mind–body relation. His work can offer a cogent starting point for my observations. He writes,

> The child reacts to this loss of an object with the attempt to regain it, to retrieve this part of himself, by imagining it . . . Attempts of this

nature continue throughout life and can be considered as the origin of the conversion process. From this point of view, it may be justifiable to broaden the concept of conversion, and above all to see in it a continually active process . . . The objects outside become reunited with the body by way of symbolisation . . . The physiologic functions of those body parts which have become the representatives of these symbolised objects are for this reason modified on account of the process of symbolisation . . . The memory symbols deposited in the body determine the character of the conversion process and also when and why it leads to a symptom formation. From this point of view the source of the symptom is the wish for, and the flight from, a symbolised object which stirs up an emotional process aimed at undoing the loss. (1959, pp. 75–76)

Due, perhaps, to intense ambivalence towards the lost but severely needed objects, the adolescent can construe these body conversions (regarded, in adults, as expressions of an acknowledged psychic identification) as extraneous, which leads to feelings of hostility and intolerance towards one's own body image and behaviour. This ambivalence can also lead to attempts at self-modifications through group identifications, which become valued self-ideals.

Thus, the actual body of the present moment—the provisional end result of an early sketch of one's relational history—must be compared with the ego-ideal that is constructed through the separation and differentiation process, to take stock of gains and losses. When adolescents repudiate aspects of themselves, they relegate them into the body, in a place experienced as alien from the self, displacing their ideal self to the social group, which is elected to be an analogon of the self. This is how the body is repudiated, split off, and becomes the container of the accrued history of the relationships with the primary objects.

Claudia, a pretty, seventeen-year-old only child, comes into analysis because she suffers from loss of appetite and gastric disorders every time she begins a sentimental relationship that risks separating her from her mother. Her mother suffers from heart disease and hypertension and uses her illness as a way to blackmail her daughter.

In a dream she brings to a session, Claudia sees herself and her mother seeking refuge on a high platform, which only they are able to reach, to escape from a lion that had escaped from the circus. She laughs when discussing the dream, saying that the tamed lion might be her father, providing her own interpretation of the family dynamics. I think that perhaps Claudia's dream expresses the manner in which she and her mother project their aggression onto Claudia's father, to avoid attacking the bond between them. This bond had become increasingly necessary since Claudia's maternal grandmother had died, as her mother had tried to nullify the loss by relying increasingly on the relationship with her daughter. Significantly, Claudia's grandmother had also suffered from heart disease and hypertension for several years, and she had had the exact same symptoms as Claudia's mother. We might read this as Claudia's mother's unconscious identification with her dead mother, and Claudia's symptoms could be seen, in turn, as unconscious identifications with the maternal bond, in conflict with her conscious desires.

In an article entitled "Le bon usage du 'matrimoine' en psychopathologie" ["About the good use of 'matrimony' in psychopathology"], Azar (1997) discusses an analogous clinical situation. She argues that the message a mother gives her own mother through her daughter is generally one of reproach, all the more resentful as it is not verbalised. (Azar provides a clinical reading of the story of Little Red Riding Hood in relation to such circular maternal relationships.) She argues that maternal inheritance (*matrimony*)—unlike the paternal inheritance of material goods, which usually occurs after death—foregrounds the transmission, during life, of immaterial and archaic qualities, which contribute to the formation of gender identity and concern a strictly feminine domain, as represented in the myth of Demeter and Kore. In the light of my own clinical work, I would add that maternal inheritance can be tantamount to incestuous desire: instead of possessing the maternal body as a sexual object, the subject possesses the "locus of conversion", which camouflages sexual desire behind its symbols.

The analytic relationship can be very accommodating to what has not been verbalised; by excluding all action, it encounters fewer obstacles in the construction of symbolic equivalents of incestuous desires. In the analytic relationship with Claudia, for example, when we begin to identify the incestuous desires camouflaged behind her concern for her mother's illness, her attitude toward sexuality gradually begins to open up. She is able to recognise certain erotic aspects of transference, which she then transforms into heterosexual forms and displaces onto objects invested in a parallel fashion.

In adolescence, the transfer of incestuous desire to the body of the analyst is a fundamental step towards the undeniable conquest of an individual identity, and an opening up to successive exchanges and displacements of primitive drive investments, which allow the fixation with the original object to be broken. In the analysis of adolescents, the analyst's bodily involvement is an essential part of the therapeutic process. The analyst must be able to relive the emotions, fears, and unconscious fantasies of her own adolescence to re-actualise them in the analytic relationship.

Jim Dine, a well-known exponent of the Pop Art movement, represents childhood as a painted starry sky, lit in one corner by a real-life child's lamp. To depict adolescence, he reddens the cheeks of a portrait of the young Rimbaud, placing the brush, stained with red paint, under the portrait. In childhood, the child's body belongs to the parents; in adolescence, the body becomes one's own domain. The artist's representation of the adolescent offers an extraordinary synthesis of the essence of two worlds, compounding an apparently angelic quality with a kind of shameful insolence. Arthur Rimbaud, the adolescent poet who declared that he wanted to experience everything, is endowed—through the act, the material gift of painting—with an emotion he was so nearly denied by the impudence of his precocious verse.

In Karen Blixen's short story *Ehrengard* (1963), the demonic painter Cazotte wishes to seduce the titular virginal warrior without touching her, by making her blush with complicity. Instead, it is the unattainable Ehrengard who makes the painter blush by translating his fantasy of seduction into an event that has already been consummated, anticipating the desire of the other.

In "Contemporary concepts on adolescent development", Winnicott maintains that

> If, in the fantasy of early growth, there is contained *death*, then at adolescence there is contained *murder* ... Growing up means taking the parent's place. It *really does*. In the unconscious fantasy, growing up is inherently an aggressive act. (2005c, p. 195)

Adolescence is a period of life in which things must be experienced. By anticipating, delaying, denying, adolescents always try to assume a position that is eccentric in relation to the other: not only do they seek their own individual identity, they must also neutralise the other's attempts to engulf it.

The mother's mirror function, Winnicott suggests, allows the child to see itself in her. Hence, every emotional deformation of the reflecting gaze has repercussions on the body and the body image deriving from it. By recovering infantile issues linked to the body as a secondary individuation process concerning sexual difference and attendant attraction, the adolescent reproduces the way in which he mirrored himself in the maternal face. Depending on the distortions and grey areas of his own image, he works through the ability to separate, the capacity to experience both what is like and unlike the self, and the ability to have "a significant exchange with the world" (Winnicott, 2005b, p. 151).

Since the way we offer ourselves to others depends on the way in which we ourselves have been seen, the teenager revives his history as fate and, at the same time, as a fight to transform it by separating from it. The body is the first other with which the adolescent grapples—it is, as Merleau-Ponty has suggested, "the sole means . . . to go unto the heart of things" (1968, p. 135).

Marina

Marina, a girl of sixteen, is an only child. She manifests all that could not occur in the mother–child relational exchange through bodily sickness. She suffers from asthma and allergies, is overweight, and continuously picks at her thin skin, which she does not feel contained by. After her childhood asthma and a struggle with bulimia, the onset of puberty, and its potential separations, has led her to focus on her body the needs and demands she failed to express to her mother. She feels that the lack of a loving relationship between her parents (who are both very disturbed) made it difficult for her to have her own affective relationships.

In the first stages of the analysis, she would often tell me she was falling to pieces and express her non-integration and integration anxieties by repeatedly touching the skin of her face. In an attempt to escape the problems arising from her difficult integration of the body, she had joined a religious sect, whose doctrine was based on elevation of the spirit and oblivion of the body. In this way, Marina could represent both her drive urgency, on the one hand, and her fantasy of being an angel, on the other. Despite being very aware of "good-looking boys", she admitted to hating men and agreed with her mother that women were superior. Marina seemed to want to avenge the fact that her mother had always felt neither beautiful nor loved. She perceived her body as a casing that did not really belong to her, as something that had scarcely been handled or cared for.

Adolescents have difficulty accepting their body image, which is deformed by the ambivalent maternal gaze. Both sexes have a tendency to see themselves as ugly and to exaggerate every small bodily imperfection. This is because omnipotence—which, in childhood, has the complicity of mutual possession and parental support—must now reckon with a world that is very often indifferent and perceived as continually threatening. The child who has been loved and cared for loves his infant body; with the advent of puberty, he no longer recognises himself in his adolescent body, because the image is competitive with his desire to remain a child. Adolescent sexuality erases the infant image to enter a dimension in which relationships must not only take into account the other's pleasure, but also the fact that this does not always coincide with our own. Integration of the body image is, therefore, a critical part of the transition into adolescence, because it involves an elaborate separation from the primary object. The teenager might even attack the body itself, at times harming it purposefully or accidentally, since the body is the root of everything—a place of nostalgia for good or insufficient care, which is rife with massive parental projections but remains, in any case, a place of separation.

Marina tends to exaggerate her affective relationship with her mother (which is openly incestuous and destructive) and deny the relationship with her father, creating an impasse and providing a container for her mother's unconscious identifications made up of hatred for her dependence on a mother who had abandoned her. Her difficulties with separation, from the maternal gaze and the constraints imposed by her incestuous desire, make it difficult for Marina to change. Her analysis proceeds slowly.

After two years of therapy, Marina dreams the body of a sick woman, sprawled and alone on the terrace of her house. Hurrying to help the woman, Marina alerts her mother that they must act fast. The body on the terrace clearly represents Marina's relationship with her mother; through this body, the patient is asking me to treat the mother's body too, in order to be able to separate from it more freely.

A thorough analysis of the dream brings a change in Marina's relationship with me and with her body. She stops picking at her skin, and her somewhat dogmatic feminist leanings, which had caused resistance to the progress of the analysis, are replaced by a healthy interest in her father and other men. She becomes attracted to a young man from northern Italy, whose regional accent is similar to mine. Voice had always exerted a container function in our analytic relationship and, with her choice and description of the man, Marina stresses its importance. Though the maternal matrix is clearly evident in this affective movement, represented by my voice, it still strikes me as important that Marina is able to invest a transformed representation of her mother. Despite its continuity with her mother, and rootedness in the maternal, this representation is strongly condensed and concealed in a shell of subsequent greater investments.

Marina's newfound romantic relationship inspires her to write poems, which are well received and published in a monthly poetry magazine. Along with the possibility of falling in love, Marina's aesthetic sensibility had also been roused. This is a form of creativity that, according to Guillaumin (1997), can serve as a container for adolescents, providing an experience that replaces other types of ideological or mystical supports aimed at transcending feelings of incompleteness and estrangement and repairing their defeats and their failures.

If one of the fundamental needs of the adolescent is to escape the desired incest, all that evokes and recalls it is evidently difficult both to pursue and to abandon. As body integration—in the sense of "maternal inheritance"—is symbolically equivalent to incestuous fulfilment and union with the mother's body, adolescence is rife with conflict. While "identificatory conversions" constitute a good use of the maternal inheritance and, therefore, continue to represent the bond with the mother's body as split identifications, body integration disregards the incestuous union, signalling that separation has occurred.

In Dostoevsky's *The Adolescent* (2004), the violent deaths of the young portray adolescence as a terrible struggle between life and death, between not wanting to die in the mother's body and not wanting to die without the life the mother has given. Above all, however, the novel tells the story of a young man in search of a paternal identity in order to build his own. To fight incestuous desires, the adolescent needs a paternal figure that does not coincide with the mother, and will not shirk from confrontation with him. In adolescence, we experience the constraints of origins, the trauma and vicissitudes of becoming. We investigate and reconstruct the bond with our origins, and feel the desire to escape from them. The adolescent wishes to inhabit a perpetual condition in which there is no solution of continuity between one's origins and becoming.

CHAPTER SIX

Adolescence as mode of mental functioning and matrix of identity

My contribution to research on adolescence, as a particular mode of mental functioning, focuses on the analytic relationship with adolescents to single out its specific characteristics. These characteristics include, for instance, the turmoil of puberty, the recourse to action in lieu of thought, the revolt against childish conservatism, which can manifest itself as transitory delusions, and a great tension towards the future. In this context, the therapist must be mindful that, when the analytic relationship contains and transforms the transference, this is not to be interpreted straightaway; it is, instead, more appropriate to give the patient the space to experience the transference and develop it in real life. Only afterwards, when sufficiently worked through, can the therapist grasp and interpret its symbolic meaning.

These remarks stem from my observation of the specific form of mental functioning that we call adolescence, and seek to generalise it as a universal human experience. Indeed, it seems to me that adolescence leaves a paradigmatic trace in all human beings, such that can be observed and analysed whatever the age of the patient, when she enters analysis. In the analysis of adult patients, in fact, it is possible to observe phenomena that are typical of the functioning of the adolescent mind, regardless of the subject's age.

It is well known that the term "adolescence" does not come from psychoanalytic theory, but stems from the need to provide a framework with which to approach the behaviour and psychological phenomena that accompany this particular biological phase of the life cycle. It is true enough that the biological parameter is rooted in the undeniable fact that puberty activates a general and complex neuronal and endocrinal constellation, whose sudden irruption and impact are so traumatic for the subject that he is wholly engaged in modifying their psychic organisation, so as to bring about significant dynamic and economic revisions. Gutton (1991) attaches much importance to the pubertal period, arguing that the term puberty relates to the body as the pubertal relates to the psyche. The creation of a word that denotes a developmental itinerary conveys both the prominence the author gives to the phenomenon and his attempt to outline the specific mode of functioning typical of this phase of life.

When adolescents have been able to acknowledge that they have been through the event of puberty, and find themselves facing the great psychic work required to process it, they often make use of the analyst as somebody to delegate to carry on some of that work—in a way reminiscent of their parents bringing them up during their childhood. If, on the one hand, the therapist has to accept this regressive need as something that is useful for the analysis, on the other she must be mindful that the overall final objective of the analysis is to help the adolescent take responsibility to carry on the work of identity construction.

Andrea—a seventeen-year-old boy, whose parents' divorce was settled in court to determine custody of the children, with allegations of the father abusing the mother—is in therapy for two years for a phobia of disease and a compulsion to wash. He has a strong desire to distance himself from such a disturbed domestic environment and experience his growing up fully and freely, and sees great therapeutic potential in the analysis. Andrea has made use of his obsessional defences to construct a provisional mode of psychic organisation, split between the infantile and the pubertal; even if this does not permit working through of his family traumata, it allows him to go through puberty as if it were a new experience, almost with no history.

Adolescents who collude with their parents and deny the pubertal event are stuck in an unavoidable infantile situation, which clashes with an external reality that becomes persecutory, in as much as the external world is the adolescents' reflecting mirror betraying their growth and attendant loss of their infantile objects. In Andrea's case, the analytic work ameliorates the persecutory aspects of reality, allowing him to gradually detach from his infantile objects and invest in his future development.

Rosy, a thirteen-year-old with bulimic tendencies, is in therapy for problems in socialising with her classmates (who make fun of her) and difficulties sleeping. At night, her two older sisters share a bed with their mother, who has separated from her husband. After a year of therapy, Rosy's attachment to the family base remains very anchored to the infantile mode and she consequently shows a lot of resistance to the real world, as if scared to leave the maternal orbit. Though sensing the need for change, the patient's ego is tied to an aspect of resistance and, therefore, expresses this need by blaming the unchanging family nucleus. The mother who shares her bed with her sisters and the father who surrounds himself with younger lovers contribute to this regressive situation against which Rosy rebels. She asks her parents to act like adults—for her father to stop chasing girls, and her mother to stop sharing her bed with her sisters—and to support and encourage her development. Family resistance ties her to the infantile, making the transition into adolescence difficult.

Teenagers find it difficult to enter an entirely different—and seemingly unattainable—perspective of identity, and this initially leads them to seek concrete, external solutions, which they may appropriate only afterwards. Gutton (2002) maintains that when the adolescent approaches puberty and intensely experiences the impact and influence of the pubertal, this does not prevent the infantile from playing a big part in determining the process and vicissitudes of adolescence. While it is true that the infantile is altered by genital change, it is also true that genitality contains the infantile traces of the subject's history.

Puberty puts to the test the ego functions and their capacity to regulate drives with behaviour adapted to reality. Although experiences of this kind occur and are often repeated in childhood, they do not acquire the intensity, quantity, and concrete bodily realisation that they do in puberty. Throughout childhood, symbolisation, sublimation, and imagination enable children to find balanced modes to process their experiences, whereas in puberty these modes are no longer sufficient, in that the pubertal subject needs concreteness, and, consequently, all forms of displacement need to be realistically meaningful and adequate. Before, condensation and symbolic equivalence were available to facilitate the economical task; in puberty, the concrete task is the work of separation and individuation. In other words, puberty proves to be a trying time for the functioning of the ego, which needs to be able to articulate the demands of internal reality with those of the external reality. In "Formulations on the two principles of mental functioning" (1911b), Freud defines this psychic function as articulation of the reality principle with the pleasure principle. In puberty, there is also some space for deferred gratification through imagination, symbolisation, and sublimation, but this possibility is predicated upon how much weight the ego has been able to give to both internal and external reality.

Although the infantile is often not available for the adolescent to recall consciously, it still orientates puberty, which, in turn, reworks the infantile. The infantile is the groove into which the pubertal fits; at the same time, puberty reshapes the infantile according to the power and strength of the available drives.

Pietro is a sixteen-year-old returning to analysis after having been in therapy with me from ages three to seven, when he had an autistic reaction to the trauma of his sister's birth. He says he remembers nothing of our previous therapeutic experience and does not want to talk about it, but his return to analysis follows a similar trauma. This time the trauma pertains to his love life: Pietro has split up with his girlfriend, who is a friend of his sister's. The event strikes me as both an attempt to break a bond that a child would only be able to set aside and an attempt to take responsibility for the trauma by engendering the painful event actively rather than experiencing it passively. When Pietro decides to terminate the therapy a year after resuming it, I have the impression that he has returned to me in order to settle the score with his mother, his therapist, and his girlfriend/sister (I return to this in greater detail in Chapters Nine and Ten).

Adolescence is, I believe, the core of life, the centre of gravity around which subjects construct their universe. This gravitational core resides in all those manifestations that we, too, hastily define pathological on account of the suffering they entail, even before adequately examining whether they are true deviations from ordinary suffering. Too often, however, we erect high-rise buildings on this centre of gravity—artificial inventions of mental functioning, all sorts of strategic compromise formations geared to the avoidance of suffering—

without which we are unable to function. Although the onset of adolescence is closely related to biological age, the same cannot be said of its development; indeed, the psychic process of adolescence and its destiny do not always coincide with biological age.

In my clinical practice, I often observe diverse and contemporaneous mental states. Indeed, even in the most disturbed patients, dynamic, representational, and ideational levels and modes of thinking oscillate between primitive modes of mental functioning and more advanced or "secondary" ones, traversing many degrees between the extreme polarities of psychic existence. Likewise, these relational modes can vary, so that fusional, autistic, narcissistic, and excessive use of projections or splitting appear side by side with aspects of separation, individuation, and object relatedness, which coherently employ secondary process functioning. One of the difficulties of psychoanalytic observation consists in distinguishing precisely and clearly between more primitive and more sophisticated or secondary levels of functioning, and assigning them to each developmental phase. In the reality of clinical practice, these diverse levels of functioning always appear and find expression at the same time.

We know that, in clinical work, we have a tendency to isolate a phenomenon, symptom, behaviour, or particular mode of operation from our overall experience with a patient, because we see it as particularly significant. We are drawn to it, not so much for the symptom's prevalence among all other manifestations, but because our singular and specific aptitude or sensibility lead us to focus particular attention on that chosen fact, which, for us, has the value of a constant conjunction of sense. Indeed, our work repeatedly calls on us to provide a point of view, but the mind's functioning cannot be understood simply from one single perspective. With regard to the modes of adolescent psychic functioning, my thoughts, thus, result from empirical reflections on what could be represented in each analysis, as the expression of a moment of crisis and adaptation.

Essentially, trauma always solicits the formation of psychic capacities that permit and enhance life, starting from the trauma of birth, which initiates the earliest forms of mental organisation. Puberty is, at the same time, the ending and the beginning of a profound transformation. It is the result of the work of recapitulation and integration of the internalised history of the subject, but it is equally the beginning of a lengthy process of reorganisation of subjectivity. It is not possible to foresee a conclusion to this process, whether it might be a natural or ideal end; rather, it is unpredictable and changeable until the very end, just as life invariably is.

The fundamental characteristic of the adolescent mind is that, in becoming aware of the power of its functioning, it recognises itself in the present, and appropriates both its past and the possibility to plan its own future. This is the typical functioning of a mind that works on two fronts, located on a strategic perspective to control and administrate two powerful psychic forces—the force aiming to confuse, and the force aiming to separate. We could say that, side by side, the death drive and life drive look toward life. This strategic perspective resembles the movement of someone who is walking backwards without losing sight of the point from which they departed. I consider this dynamic position to be the most integrated mode of functioning, straddling the border between Eros and Thanatos, where the adolescent can mitigate omnipotence and find new ways of negotiating conflicts. Once this process of profound reorganisation is well under way, we can say that the subject has got through a piece of adolescence and has attained a sufficiently stable identity, one that can be flexible and adapt to concrete occurrences and needs.

Providing a reliable physio-pathological framework of adolescence is by no means a simple matter. It would, in fact, be more appropriate to speak of the manifestation of two opposing tendencies, which are the combination of multiple factors and operate on two fronts: on one side, the need to destabilise and call into question the current mode of functioning; on the other, a different structuring need, both conservational and transformational, aimed at creating new psychic capacities apt to carry out new tasks.

Adolescents who feel profoundly caught between the part of the self that maintains the bond with its origin and the self that seeks separateness, individuation, and self-assertion work incessantly to manage the opposing pressures coming from both fronts. To be able to carry on the work, the mind oscillates between functions, positions, and mechanisms that have been previously learnt and subsequently reinforced by the events of new traumata, which have rendered them ever more efficient and sophisticated. Examples in point are the schizoid, paranoid, or depressive constellations, which—together with splitting, withdrawal, and isolation—are forms that cannot ever be entirely relinquished or overcome, and remain, instead, as latent and always possible modes of mental functioning. This is how adolescents process their experience, perennially on the verge of madness and death.

Through all these oscillations, the separate self-representation and the confused self-representation are no longer felt to be radically incompatible, but begin to exist in a plausible relationship. I contend that human beings need to employ all of these mental states, which they must learn how to link and articulate, as legitimate possibilities available for their functioning. This is a somewhat different position from privileging a "normal" state, as my emphasis resides instead particularly on the organic collaboration of states.

Adolescence can also be regarded as the individual's first decision to live, after the original decision to give life made by the parents. This is a decision to leave behind the original psychotic condition, which is dissociated and split off, and take responsibility for the shape of one's own existence. Beginning from the original omnipresent condition, adolescents traverse the triadic–oedipal vicissitudes, and then move towards a situation in which they can think of themselves as essentially alone in the world.

I do not believe that the adolescent crisis can ever be "grown out of". It is always rediscovered in all adult analyses. The only real transformation I observe in adults, as opposed to adolescent predicaments, concerns the recourse to action. In adults, a large quantity of actions are represented and not carried through: the quantity of energy available for discharge, from infancy through adolescence, and into adulthood, is gradually transformed into more symbolic processes. Indeed, the recourse to action is a distinctively adolescent phenomenon, not only as an economical mechanism to relieve tension, but, above all, as the quickest path to representation, aimed at recovering largely repressed or repudiated and unbearable contents, in a way that does not burden the ego excessively.

This is why adolescents absorbed in their crises are still remarkably capable of insight—not in the sense of attaining awareness, but, rather, of intuiting and repeating. With their quick and sharp illuminations that lead to rapid actions, adolescents go through sudden changes of course and act in impulsive and non-thought-out ways, while all the time "making sense". The importance of this action resides in its functioning as a bridge between representations that are still linked to unconscious phantasies and potential representations that are yet to be verbalised, but have already reached communication. To act means to stage one's personal experiences and affects in the world, so as to be able to acknowledge and appropriate them in the symbolic register.

Nowadays, we tend to consider the adolescent predicament as a natural, rather than a pathological, crisis. It is true, however, that the entity, intensity, and violence of this crisis can easily turn into a traumatic potential for serious psychopathology. Adolescence is a time when a significant reality testing occurs and the adolescent must reckon with his capacity to deal with it. Sometimes, adolescents have psychotic breakdowns, at times they kill themselves or die prematurely, and at times they employ all their resources to avoid the perilous experience of adolescence altogether. In the latter scenario, a developmental arrest occurs, and the subject freezes the drama of adolescence but also his own developmental potential (although the adolescent work can later be resumed, at more appropriate times).

This is why many authors suggest that genuine adolescent psychopathology essentially concerns the capacity to enter adolescence and go through puberty. The core issue, here, is facing the tragic sense of limit, which sometimes feels unacceptable—the limits, for example, of accepting sexual difference, of loss, and the finitude of life itself. When this developmental stumbling block does not precipitate a florid psychotic regression, what frequently happens is that the adolescent finds a solution in remaining on the developmental level reached, settling into a condition where there are small forward movements that stave off both the regressive pull and the developmental drive. This mode of mental functioning—which resembles a sort of waiting game—is a paradigmatic one for adolescents who have not yet given up on their existential odyssey (and is also often the state of things that adult patients present when they come into analysis). This particular mode holds the subject on the threshold—between progression and regression, separateness and union, without reaching definition or delimitation—settled in a place from which it is possible to lean forward without moving, neither entering the new, nor fully leaving the old.

This is an acquired survival strategy, a form of adaption that the adolescent has learnt and will not easily relinquish. It is essentially a borderline defensive strategy, which becomes established with fitting effectiveness to prevent the ego from experiencing violent conflicts, and this might well be the reason why this defence can be mobilised during traumatic crises. Searles (1994) goes so far as to state that the borderline defence is fundamental throughout life, that we probably learn it in its rudimentary form in childhood, and consolidate it when the impact of the adolescent crisis becomes apparent. Green (1996) describes it as a "no man's land".

The capacity for splitting, multiple identifications, the stalling of regressive pulls and progressive drives, the holding on to a centre of gravity—these are all strategic devices that permit the subject to be everywhere and nowhere at once. Life and mental sanity are what is at stake, but the price to pay is the sacrifice of personal identity. This is a form of functioning construed in order to avoid the danger of being entrapped by both external reality and internal objects, and also as a protection from the fear of rejection and of actively rejecting one's own desires. In other words, the subject pays the price of not being able to construct an identity suited to the self, in as much as they are afraid of losing it.

My clinical experience has led me to conclude that the essential aim of analysis with these patients is not to carry out the work of identity straight away. I do not, therefore, consider it useful to interpret or verbalise needs, desires, libidinal or destructive objects and aims, either from the past or in the here and now of the therapeutic relationship, even when the opportunity arises during the session. The rationale behind this choice is that interpreting this material would only reinforce the patient's mistrust, intensifying resistance to a relationship that is already overcharged with expectations. If anything, a theoretically astute therapeutic choice would be to favour the adolescent's experience of the analytic relationship as a relationship with an object that does not impose, overwhelm, seduce, or attract drive investments with the promise that they will, at long last, be satisfied. In other words, a subject whose identity is still immature needs a therapist with a solid identity, someone who has confidence in the therapeutic method and does not need to be found and used as an object straightaway. I would say that the most favourable environment is one in which the therapist can wait and support the adolescent patient, whose task it is to broaden the functions of the ego with which the analyst should entertain a dialectic rapport. "The analytic device contributes to making space in time", writes Chianese (2006, p. 45, translated for this edition).

It creates a space that is "psychic" as well as "relational". In this space we see the formation and display of "geometries" and "figures" that are both unconscious "figures" and possible configurations of the analytic relationship, to which both analyst and patient contribute.

In a paper entitled "On not interpreting", Bonaminio argues that

Winnicott's concept of holding, which discriminates between the function of the mother as environment and her position as object, appears to me to be more useful clinically, because it allows more room to describe those moments in the analysis when the analyst's presence has not yet become that of an object for the patient. Holding is subtly distinguished from handling and from object presenting as a function of the "mother's primary concern", metaphorically referable to "therapeutic concern", a founding aspect when taking a patient into care. The first two, holding and handling, referable to spontaneous maturational processes of integration and personalisation, constitute the mother's silent contribution (the therapist's not interpreting) which upholds the child's germinative Self. The more active presenting object (just as the interpreting function is active) can, on the other hand, be seen as a kind of bridge which . . . sparks off the relationship by way of projective identification . . . as a successive modality which structures both. (1993, p. 88)

There is no psychoanalytic or technical reason why the therapist should collude with the persecutory aspects of the patient, and this would certainly occur if the therapist were to impose the individuation process in a way that would threaten the therapeutic process. When patients have had a sufficiently reliable experience of a non-competitive relational setting, which does not predefine their identity, they will then begin to transfer aspects of the self, aspects of relationships that have not yet been integrated, and repudiated part-objects. Only then will they begin to acknowledge their own needs and desires, on the one hand, and the qualities of the object, on the other. It is at this point that the real analytic work begins. I think that, first and foremost, the experience and creation of time is necessary in order to be able to relinquish infantile omnipotence and access the domains of "possibility" and "limit".

CHAPTER SEVEN

Psychopathology of the process of the work of identity: resistance and loneliness when aggression is turned into masochism

When adolescents prolong the difficulties of childhood into the pubertal age, they are confronted by another difficulty they are not ready to face—sexuality and sexual identity. In such situations, the teenager is forced to subjugate sexuality to the omnipotent defensive purposes organised in childhood, rather than expressing it and using it to enrich identity. Since genuine sexual desire signals that successful separation has occurred, if an omnipotent state of non-separation must be defended this most frequently gives rise to frigidity in women and impotence in men. Anorexia and bulimia, for example, are pathologies that mainly concern the feminine and are closely connected with the difficulty of accepting a defined sexual identity.

"We possess nothing in the world", wrote Weil, "a mere chance can strip us of everything—except the power to say 'I'" (2002, p. 26). Weil was a philosopher, political activist, and intellectual who died of consumption and hardship in 1943 aged thirty-four, after a life spent defending her ideals. Like a medieval ascetic, she refused to attribute any importance to the body, writing in her *Notebooks* that "we must desire nothing" (2004, p. 421). Weil's statements and behaviours make me think of the anorexic patients I have treated, but also bring to mind a common and widespread refusal of all that which girls must endure in order to become women.

It is precisely because chance can deprive the subject of everything—perhaps even of the capacity to assert the "I"—that the anorectic patient clamours that she needs "nothing" in order to make the "I" statement. Her self-assertion can only come to fruition through displacement: the anorectic is fixated to the logic of absolutes; therefore, she can only make an investment on the ideal self in relation to an ideal object. This construction is predicated upon the splitting of the real and the ideal and the attendant displacement of the self and object onto an ideal context.

To want nothing emphasises the lack of the dialectic of desire, which functions according to an all-or-nothing logic, and to want nothing lays a radical claim to everything. The perspective underlying this is one of a fundamental division into two components: the right to have everything, and the frustration of this basic entitlement remaining unfulfilled. In *Family Complexes in the Formation of the Individual* (2003), Lacan calls it the larva's desire. With this constructive mode of relating to reality, the histories that patients narrate almost always fit this defensive process.

Nadia

Nadia is eighteen years old, very beautiful, and incredibly thin. She has an axe to grind about two things in particular—the first is her mother's decision not to speak to her in her native tongue; the other is an obsession with her very dynamic elder sister, who is a constant obstruction to the total possession of her mother. It was Nadia's sister who encouraged her to seek analysis, though it is unclear how exactly this took place. Nadia fears that analysis will jeopardise the construction she had made of her life—she seems to want to slip through life unseen, by me as well. She is pleased with her amenorrhea and her ability to eat very little, just enough to allow her to function and study. On the one hand, coming into analysis seems a way for her to express a need silently; on the other, perhaps, she fantasises about the analysis providing an opportunity to create her own ideal context for her anorexic modes.

If the analytic situation can generally be considered one of omnipotence, this is certainly true for anorectics—to the degree that it might be used as a non-transformable experience. The anorectic needs an object for her illness, which, in itself, is not an object to be treated, since anorectic behaviour is the patient's way of asserting the "I". To this end, anorectics constantly need to seduce without ever wanting to be seduced. This becomes possible when the analytic encounter avails itself of the analyst's simultaneous need to recreate this particular relational mode.

In one session, Nadia brings me some short stories she has been writing and her diary to read, and shows me the earrings she designed and made herself. The sole purpose of this ostensible seduction is to put me to the test. In a previous session, she had told me about her habit of having lunch at the pizzeria next door to my consulting room, where she would eat a very small slice of pizza. Initially, she said, she found the owners pleasant and had befriended them; soon after, however, she had felt increasingly sought-after and subjected to excessive attentions and had stopped going there. Her story warned me against reciprocating her seductiveness, even if this requires a lot of attention and commitment on my part. In the therapy, Nadia seeks to make herself loved, without wanting to understand that someone might actually take her up on her wish.

One of her short stories—which I find very beautiful and also intriguing—seems, in some way, to represent the dynamics of how she had experienced her family history. The story is about two cousins—one of whom sick with leukaemia—who love and hate each other, as they are both in love with the same boy. Both of the cousins' families are composed of overworked fathers and depressed mothers. Nadia is clearly using the story to talk about her own family, and her very close relationship with her sister who, she suggests, had stolen the object of her affections. In actual fact, Nadia's sister's boyfriend had initially courted her, but she had always refused his advances. She did this with everyone she desired, being wary of explicit feelings that the other might correspond and render concrete, thus potentially upsetting her position of dominance.

As Recalcati writes in *L'ultima cena: anoressia e bulimia* [The Last Supper: Anorexia and Bulimia], anorexia–bulimia is not a structure but, rather, "a phenomenon that, for some of its specific characteristics—seriality, discursive monotony, identificatory rigidity, exalted narcissism—tends to conceal rather than reveal the structure of the subject" (1997, p. 193, translated for this edition). In the case in hand, it seems that Nadia is concealing a hysterical structure under her anorectic discourse. "The anorectic", Recalcati continues, "denies herself as object of fulfilment to acquire the phallic value of an object valued precisely because it can never be entirely possessed". Nadia's behaviour suggests a lack in her mother's desire, which has always been directed elsewhere—to the father, her distant brother, her elder daughter, her condition as a foreigner in Italy. All this, however, probably stands for her inability to be in contact with a primitive and extremely dependent aspect of the self. Nadia identifies with this lack, thereby establishing a non-transformable bond with the maternal object. In the analysis, she is concerned that a different relational mode might be created between us—she is afraid, that is, of being able to be the object of care and desire.

After the first year of analysis at three sessions per week, Nadia tells me that she dreamed she had gone to a supermarket and bought a large jar of low-calorie jam. She says she was very happy because she could eat this jam without feeling stuffed. I remark that this is perhaps what she wants from me; she adds, with a smile, that she wants a low-calorie analysis.

The large jar of dietetic jam contains a copious quantity that is readily available but does not compel its consumption, not even out of greed. Indeed, as it is a dietary measure, the lack of calories attenuates greed. The offer, here, is free from the violence of the other's narcissistic desire, which always imposes as an absolute good, to be consumed in its entirety. Perhaps this is the act of love that anorectics ask of the other: to renounce narcissistic desire in order to reciprocate their weak and limited desire, which is always frustrating for the other. The anorectic's need is as tenuous as her desire—and if it is flooded by desire for the other's life, it kills the glimmer of life that can be born in her.

Interpretation, as it is usually considered, plays first and foremost to the analyst's need to complete a process, to not feel powerless before the patient. Nadia made me realise how important it was for her that I should not go over her head, that I offer her only points of connection rather than certainties. Imagination and dream play a particularly indispensable role with those patients who need to be free to ask, without always being offered something in return, before their desire can emerge.

On the when and how of interpretation, it is useful to quote Thanopulos:

> The work of interpretation in analysis is constantly inspired by a process of cross-phantasising which brings analysand and analyst together on an equal footing. In giving focus to the phantasy of the other the analyst also, indirectly, gives configuration to his own. This requires no awareness on the part of the interpreting subject; instead, it derives from the principle of psychic continuity. (2005, p. 405)

For a long time, the analytic relationship with Nadia carries on like this, in a manner that is subdued but resistant, despite its lightness. Always being on the cusp of rupture is precisely what guarantees continuity in our relationship, as is desirable in any case of anorexia.

Romano, author of *An Invented Youth*, once said, "For young people, life is a compromise between being and existing. That is why youth is tragic" (1979, p. 282, translated for this edition). Romano's words bring to mind the fate of anorectics, who must continually risk their existence in order to be. At times, anorexia and bulimia provide a provisional mode in which the adolescent crisis manifests itself.

Maria

Maria is a very graceful fifteen-year-old girl. The fantastic narrations she shares in our sessions are deeply imbued with events from her family life. Her parents are separated, and her brother once had an accident at sea, which he only narrowly survived. She is small in stature and tending to obesity, and her father, who is tall and lean, has begun to make fun of her for being overweight. The strong anger provoked by her father's words arouses an equally competitive determination to lose weight and be thinner. She has started to eat very little and has lost a lot of weight, and had a spell of amenorrhea, which attracted the concerns of her family. Maria tells me that she experienced this period of extreme thinness as a recovery of substance, feeling finally that she had become someone. Tempting death felt as if she was touching life. After this initial period of thinness, Maria has been overwhelmed by the constant attention her family pay to her eating habits, which oscillate from a single salad leaf to binges on biscuits that leave her feeling humiliated and guilty. It is at this time that she seeks psychotherapy, at two sessions a week, spurred on by her mother's fears. Her mother accuses her father of indifference, and even of having encouraged Maria to put two fingers down her throat in a moment of bulimic frenzy.

In therapy, through her own narrations, Maria begins to feel that she is actually surrounded by people who have similar problems to her. Her father, who cares deeply about maintaining a perfect physique, goes to the gym every day; her mother, brother, and grandmother are constantly on a diet. Maria's grandmother, in particular, talks continually about all the food she is depriving herself of, while her brother's diet seems to have temporarily placated his anxiety issues.

Unlike the rest of her family, Maria refuses to go on a diet, as this would mean accepting that someone impose something on her. In our sessions, she talks extensively about food; at times, she also mentions, in passing, how committed she is to her schoolwork and music lessons. Her mood varies, depending on whether she has been able to refrain from eating entirely, or has eaten a plateful of biscuits, shifting between feelings of euphoric omnipotence typical of anorectic behaviour and the depressive tendencies of bulimia. Her attitude towards me largely reflects how she is feeling about herself: she is kind and affectionate when she can refrain from eating, but treats me with hatred and contempt when she gorges on food. This also depends, it must be said, on the development of the analytic relationship: if the analyst is seductive or intrusive, Maria is more prone to bulimia and, consequently, to hatred; if the analyst is able to contain herself and be easily manipulated by the patient, Maria displays a sense of omnipotence and gratitude. This type of patient certainly does not dependably follow the rhythm of sessions—rather, the trend fluctuates depending on her feelings of self-affirmation, as a form of out-and-out resistance.

As is often the case during early adolescence, Maria's dreams share the fundamental characteristic of being highly condensed. In the first dream that she brings, a child is born and immediately requires heart surgery. Naturally, I presume this is related to the enormous risk Maria associates with the analysis, but it also suggests how adept she is at threatening others and making them feel guilty—strategies to render the object inert and easy to manipulate. It is almost as if she is saying, any slight movement on your part is enough to kill me. In her associations to this dream, Maria says that perhaps the child with the sick heart needs a lot of love—her words suggest an awareness of the violence of love as it is represented in her dream.

In a second dream, of a few months later, a woman armed with a gun is chasing her and her brother in a park. The woman finally manages to catch up with them and reveals to them that their father has another family. The dream allows Maria to discuss her childhood fantasies about her parents' relationship, on which she evidently projected her anxieties of ambivalence and unreliability. In her eyes, neither her mother nor her father was able to embody a maternal or paternal function, and no object seemed reliable enough to identify with it. This explains Maria's need to dwell on the margins, perched on the threshold of a relationship that could neither be investigated more thoroughly, nor introjected. The tension of ambivalence was held at its highest point to remain always on edge between the untouchable condition of omnipotence and the contamination of introjection.

A third dream, several months later, appears to suggest that Maria is becoming more involved in the analysis. In her dream, the patient walks into a restaurant with her mother and brother, and finds herself face to face with a woman whose appearance—which resembled a homeless person's—frightens her. Maria speaks at length about her problems with food and how each time she eats too much she feels degraded. "Like a homeless person", I add, and she agrees, saying that is precisely the reason why it is important to know how to resist.

In the following period, Maria feels more positive and constructive, because she is able to dominate her needs. Feeling more self-confident, she has also found a boyfriend. In anorexia–bulimia, the extreme difficulty with experiencing conflict gives rise to splitting that deepens and propagates with every experience. We could trace this back to a primitive inability to reconcile the experience of presence with the experience of absence, which later spreads to all the polarities of psychic life: love–hate, fullness–emptiness, male–female, body–mind. Difficulties with symbolising continuity in discontinuity (as many have argued) or in sensory or representative oscillation (I would add) cause this rift to open up rather than close down.

Anorectic–bulimic organisation appears linked to an experience of "betrayal", or early disappointment, to use Winnicott's model. Therefore, I believe (in slight disagreement with those Lacanians who have addressed the matter extensively) that it is not that anorectics–bulimics have an experience of fullness or emptiness in their past, but, rather, that they have an experience of early fullness that has been interrupted abruptly.

In the correspondence of the anorexic saint, Catherine of Siena, we find an intriguing letter to her niece, dated 1379. In it, Catherine writes,

> And you see that of yourself you are not, and because you are not, you see that you cannot help yourself and so with faith you run to the One who is. He can help you in your every need, and he knows how to and wants to . . . Where will you strip yourself of the selfish love that makes you impatient when you are hurt or suffer in other ways, and clothe yourself in a divine love that will make you patient and glory in the cross of Christ crucified? . . . We receive and enjoy this mother, prayer, more or less perfectly depending on how we feed on the angelic food, holy and true desire for God, rising up high . . . to eat it at the table of the most holy cross . . . I long to see you feeding on the food of angels, because I don't see how else you can be a true spouse of Jesus Christ, consecrated to him in holy religious life. (2008, p. 195)

Compounding the metaphors of nourishment and eating, emptiness and plenitude, Christ is also a figure for the crucifixion of the bodily self—a body that can no longer express the subject's needs as a result of a disappointment: a body that, of itself, is not.

"If the child is to become adult", writes Winnicott, "then this move is achieved over the dead body of an adult (I must take it for granted that the reader knows that I am referring to unconscious fantasy, the material that underlies playing)" (2005a, pp. 195–196). When speaking of their adolescent children, countless parents describe the long hard labour they must endure in living with them. Their anxiety is often expressed along these lines: "When they were small, sickness of the body were what worried us most; now that they have grown up, their suffering seems deeper, like an invisible pain of the soul". Some parents speak perceptively of their children's psychic suffering during adolescence, of the sadness into which they see them sink, and the irritation they feel when they cannot separate from them (irritation that often turns into violence). Aggression in adolescence is palpable in all behaviour because the subject's desires are so contradictory that they engender endless internal struggles.

Bernhard writes poetically and ironically on this subject, under the guise of an eternal adolescent, in his memoir, *Gathering Evidence*. "We are brought forth, but we are not brought up", he writes,

> Having brought us forth, our procreators proceed to treat us with all the mindless ineptitude it requires to destroy the new human being they have made. During the first three years of his life they contrive to ruin whatever potential he was born with, not knowing the least thing about him—except perhaps that he was produced unthinkingly and irresponsibly—and not realising that in producing him they were committing the greatest possible crime. Having brought us into the world in sheer *base ignorance*, our procreators—that is, our parents—are at a loss to know how to deal with us once we are there. All their attempts at dealing with us end in failure, and they soon give up, though never soon enough—never before they have succeeded in destroying us ... The new human beings born into the world, their education is bound to lead to their ruin ... This all takes place in the very first days, weeks, months, and years of the child's life, for what he receives and perceives in this early period determines what he will be and what he will remain throughout his life. (2010, pp. 111–112)

In all likelihood, the function of this hyperbolic language, typical of the delusional teenager, is to amplify the power of opposition and separation—to compensate, in other words, for the subject's feelings of powerlessness. This is typical of the teenager who experiences his fate as unjust, and lays his claim to the "good inheritance" he was owed but not given. Bernhard's words also emphasise the great truth of just how important the first days, months, and years of life really are.

As Winnicott claims, if the child cannot experience the destruction—without retaliation—of the object, she cannot successfully use that object. The object has value when it survives the child's ruthlessness: "the subject can now *use* the object that has survived" (2005a, p. 121). The subject's big test is being able to find a bastion on to which to direct his aggressiveness, and, consequently, begin to trust that his badness can be contained. Aggression and sadism are part of human nature, but all excesses of these arise from the fact that at times our natural expression cannot be tolerated and accepted (just as the person who is not listened to shouts to call the object back to its function). In many cases, adolescents in therapy describe very painful childhood situations, revealing the helplessness (*Hilflosigkeit*) of the new-born baby, or parents who diligently supply their children and teenagers with material goods without listening to their psychic suffering. As I have stressed above, in a certain period of life this suffering becomes essential and is much more important than any material possessions.

It is useful, here, to consider the cases of two young patients of mine, whose destructive behaviour particularly struck me. I believe that in the situations I will describe "pre-integration aggression" has not had an effective protective shield; in the "stage of concern" the subject's strong feelings of guilt towards the mother could not be tolerated, rendering the personal need to give, build, and repair unattainable (Winnicott, 2001c[1950]).

Rita

Rita is a girl of about twenty, who has led a very difficult life. She lost her father in a car accident when she was three years old. Her father, who was an important politician, was also survived by a previous partner and the children they had had together. Rita's mother and father were not married, their family life was rather precarious, and relations were a little turbulent. Rita's brother, Simone, was born a year after her, and the family nucleus would perhaps have been strengthened by the arrival of a second child, had the fatal accident not occurred.

After the death, insecurity becomes the family's defining feature, engendering feelings of loneliness and abandonment. The violent loss and lack of the father creates a sense of fear and anxiety that spread to all aspects of life. The mother—a very fragile and depressive woman, who had already been rather absent in the first years of her children's lives—begins to shift the grief she could not work through on to the children. She becomes tyrannical, especially with Rita.

Rita is not allowed to stay out late; when she goes out alone, her mother insists she phone her constantly, to quell her fears that something might happen to her. Rita describes the anger and frustration she felt as a child and then as a teenager as everything she attempted ended in failure: her school, friendships, and sentimental relationships. Instead of expressing her feelings, she kept everything inside, and this unconsciously worked against her, inhibiting her creative potential. During Rita's childhood, her mother's pervasive fear and insecurities led her to react to life in much the same way: she, too, was afraid of everything—especially of losing her mother, the family's sole support. She would often awake in a panic from nightmares that primarily represented the event of a traumatic loss. Clearly, these were dreams of castration, in which the death drive triumphed.

When Rita first comes to therapy, she tells me she has had my address in her pocket for two years, but could not make up her mind to contact me; she was afraid of seeking treatment, of recognising that she needed help. She talks to me about her recent difficulties in graduating from secondary school and her abortive attempts to enrol in university. She is currently living alone, though her boyfriend often stays over, taking advantage of her hospitality. Occasionally, she works as a sales assistant, and her mother helps her out financially. She tells me she has a rather difficult relationship with people in general, often feeling exploited by them. For example, she always lends money when people—especially men—ask her to. The problem has got worse over the years—to the point that Rita now feels that if she does not give people money, they will not want to spend time with her.

Rita's words remind me of a passage from "The economic problem of masochism" (1924c). "It is very tempting in explaining this attitude", Freud writes, "to leave the libido out of account and to confine oneself to assuming that in this case the destructive instinct has been turned inwards and is now raging against the self". But analysis with Rita reveals that under her goody-goody veneer lies a profound sense of guilt, which, for Freud, "is perhaps the most powerful bastion in the subject's (usually composite) gain from illness – in the sum of forces which struggle against his recovery and refuse to surrender his state of illness" (1924c, pp. 165–166).

A dream Rita brings me after a year of therapy features a couple violently torturing each other, just like in Roman Polanski's film *Bitter Moon*. The duality of the couple, I think, permits each partner to occupy a pole of the sadism–masochism spectrum, and, thus, avoid taking responsibility for the other. In any case, the fundamental advantage afforded by oscillating between these two polarities is the attenuation of guilt—either because one partner prevalently plays the role of the victim, or because the other is complicit, hence guilty, so the union can become a mode of mutual compensation for guilt.

This is why Winnicott sees killing as equivalent to being killed (putting the onus on aggressiveness, rather than the way in which it presents itself). "Being weak is as aggressive as the attack of the strong on the weak", he writes. "Murder and suicide are fundamentally the same thing. Perhaps most difficult of all, possession is as aggressive as is greedy acquisition" (2001c[1950], p. 204).

In her daily life, Rita typically takes on the role of the victim, and she also behaves in analysis in a passive, self-pitying way. Being the victim is an attempt to erase the guilt instilled in her since she was a child by a mother who was extremely possessive and terrified of reality. I perceive a strong anger rising in me as Rita tells me about her behaviours—especially in her amorous and sexual relations, in which she allows herself to be treated violently by the boy whom she is seeing and who is currently living with her. The situation seems so extreme that I am unable to identify with her, even to the minimal degree that understanding usually implies. Most of the time, however, I realise that I am the victim and she is the torturer. This reversal of roles is a collusive solution to the relationship's economical malaise, and not yet an understanding or working through; despite remaining implicit, it does, however, bring about a change and is the starting point of a slow but gradual new awareness.

One day, for instance, Rita skips a session—something that is unthinkable for her. On the one hand, I feel sadistically relieved; on the other, I am left alone to play the role of the victim. In the following session, Rita admits to being terrified by the idea that I will rebuke her severely for missing her session and make her leave the consulting room. These are precisely the same reactions that, as a child, she feared from her mother. The fact that she is now able to imagine that the therapist has survived her attack and has, in fact, accepted it serenely is the condition for the transformation of her relationship with the object. She can begin to tolerate guilt without feeling like a criminal, because omnipotence is no longer just a characteristic of the negative, but also of the positive.

Anna

Anna is a very pretty nineteen-year-old girl. She is in therapy twice a week for acute symptoms that cause her a great deal of distress. She is obsessed by all the women whom her current boyfriend might find attractive, and especially by certain parts of her body: her breasts, bottom, and legs. Anna had her first boyfriend aged fourteen, though her parents did not approve of her choice because the boy's family was not well off. Their relationship had been happy but she had eventually broken it off, at her parents' insistence. At sixteen, she had met another boy, and it was with him that her jealous obsession for other women first emerged. Her behaviour became so extreme that it led to violence from both parties, to the point that some episodes landed them in Accident and Emergency. For these reasons, the relationship ended dramatically.

Towards the end of secondary school, Anna meets Luca, her current boyfriend. Some way into their relationship, she begins to feel maddeningly jealous. She is afraid that Luca will be interested in other women's bodies, and torments him for hours asking him to reassure her that this is not the case. In truth, it is Anna who is obsessed with other women, and especially with extreme sexual behaviour involving them.

After I suggest to Anna that we seek the root of her obsessions in her childhood, she recounts many episodes from her past, interspersed with dreams, in which her family nucleus appears very closed and ensnared. Anna is an only child; and though her parents heaped all their expectations for intellectual and professional success on her, she says they always appeared a little cold and distant, to the point that, as a child, she imagined she had been adopted. Anna's mother, a very beautiful and depressive woman, quit her job when Anna was small to take care of her sick parents, who then died in close succession.

Around the time she recounts these episodes from her past, Anna dreams that she has a baby, whom she first forgets in her cellar, and then takes for a stroll with her mother towards the cemetery. The melancholic atmosphere that reigns in Anna's stories is given mainly by feelings of emptiness, a void in her childhood experiences. The death of her grandparents, and their long illness before that, formed the background of Anna's childhood; her mother's desolation at her grandmother's death was perhaps the cause of the emotional coldness that I could perceive in Anna's behaviour. Ever since her childhood, she appears to have defended herself by immersing herself in an atmosphere of masturbatory excitement.

The dream child she takes on a stroll with her mother towards the cemetery could represent her childhood history, and her fantasies of sexual arousal would, thus, be her way of protecting herself from the void of nothingness. Anna's melancholy relates to a pre-mirror stage impossibility of forming an image of herself, a failure in the maternal mirroring function. "What does the baby see when he or she looks at the mother's face?" asks Winnicott. "I am suggesting that, ordinarily, what the baby sees is himself or herself . . . Many babies, however, do have to have a long experience of not getting back what they are giving. They look and they do not see themselves" (2005b, p. 151). In this light, Cupelloni (2002) argues that the singularity of the melancholic state indicates the particular way in which every psychic life encounters and works through the experience of the death of the fantasy of the other. For her, this working through is inherently bound to the subject's specific identity, be they boy or girl, man or woman, in a determined culture and time.

In the early stages of therapy, Anna would say, "Enjoy work!" at the end of our sessions, as her way of saying goodbye. When I bring this up one day, she says she is happy that I have commented on this and that it annoys me, because it is her way of highlighting the professional distance between us. Around that time, she dreams that she must eat frozen bread; I observe that perhaps she has the feeling that, in therapy, she is being administered cold, tasteless food. After these incidents, Anna asks if she can remain seated during our sessions, because she wants to look at me—this makes it easier for her to imagine I am not getting distracted. I agree to her request and, from that moment, feel that the perceptual function, which until then was very repressed, acquires a fundamental value in the relationship—almost as if the object had given her permission to look at it, so she no longer had to ask for it from others (such as her boyfriend). It seems to me that from this moment a greater mutual intimacy is established.

Anna tells me that when she feels very bad, she masturbates to fantasies about her boyfriend looking at sexily dressed women. Around this time, her dreams are frequently of an erotic nature. One night, she dreams about television showgirl Alba Parietti stripping and wakes up with cramp in one of her legs. Another night, she dreams she is watching hard-core pornography on television with a seven-year-old child. In relating these dreams, she angrily calls the other's desire into question, and I suspect that Anna is disguising her desire for women with her interest in men. Yet, it is almost as if she is lost in the constant refusal of the request for love, as if to say, "How could anyone desire me when such images exist?"; "What hope do I have when all these goods are on offer?"

When she grills boyfriend Luca on his feelings for her—something she admits to doing "like a criminal"—she feels "alive, meaningful". The rest of the time she feels absent, as if her obsession were the only thing able to provide her with an identity. The need to look is very important for Anna—this is why she asked to face me, and her large girlish eyes seem to want to devour the image of me, to possess all that she projects onto me. When I consider her fantasies and dreams, I relate them to her jealousy of the maternal body; indeed, as a child, Anna was very jealous of her parents' relationship, above all of her mother. On one occasion, she had entered her parents' bedroom and had found them semi-naked. Perhaps this memory expresses her attachment to a highly exciting primal scene that painfully feeds her incestuous fantasies and the need to confine them to an obsessive symptom.

In discussing the cases of these two girls, Anna and Rita, I have stressed their pathological impossibility, extending into late adolescence, of freely expressing their emerging sexual identity. This is almost an acknowledgment of the difficulties in separating from the incestuous bond with the mother and the omnipotence associated with it.

CHAPTER EIGHT

Vicissitudes of identity and marriage

Although the infantile organisation of identity has its economy, allowing the ego to defend itself, for the most part, from the sexual and aggressive taboos linked to the subject's culture and times, adulthood brings this economy into crisis. While it is legitimate for children to defend themselves from sexuality, this is not the case for adults. As seen in previous chapters, it is by no means easy for teenagers to begin an autonomous and adequate sentimental life, precisely because such relationships put strain on their primitive defences against sexuality. When contemplating sexuality within the framework of a relationship that, by nature, is familial, the subject is forced to reorganise the whole infantile defence system, which is not always an easy task.

Marriage is a rite and a symbol—a stage that is not always easily reached, due to the deep and unconscious link all human beings entertain with the original taboo of incest. In traditional rituals, the sacred serves to forgive original sin and legitimate sexuality with the aim of procreation. The ties symbolised in the rite, however, are not only of a religious nature—rather, religious ties can, at times, provide an alibi or a front for deeper psychological, unconscious ties. In Catholic culture, marriage is one of the seven sacraments. With the other six, the individual passively receives so-called sacramental grace to strengthen the spirit; in marriage, however, the sacramental substance lies in the responsibility of the two parties involved, as, by saying "I do", they enter the sacred and perform an act of mutual acceptance of their natures and histories.

Rituals of this nature can facilitate the working through of difficulties related to sexuality. However, reaching the point where the rite of marriage may be celebrated presupposes that the subject has been able to process the experience of the primal scene and that some form of identification with this experience has taken place.

Marriage, as it is presented in Blixen's *On Modern Marriage and Other Observations* (1987), no longer has the dramatic, grievous characteristics of Tolstoy's *The Kreutzer Sonata and Other Stories* (1985) or *Anna Karenina* (2016), and less and less frequently in the Western world does the sacrament emblematise a fate imposed by parents on their children. In her book, Blixen asks what transforms an immoral relationship between man and woman into a moral one; the answer she comes up with is love. Even marriage today—which has the law on its side, and can be undone at the slightest infringement of fidelity—may still be seen as a relationship of love.

As I have said, marriage might, at times, be difficult to achieve, but it is often difficult to undo. Its ritual nature likens it to experiences of separation, mourning, and loss of a previous condition, therefore (as with all changes resulting from even slight transformation) it is difficult both to enter into and emerge from. Marriage can, thus, be thought of as a symbol of the original union, of the sense of omnipotent wholeness which has been transferred to our parents and which one can have the fantasy of reappropriating. At the same time, however, the infantile position of being a child to the parental couple is lost, along with adolescent anarchic rebellion against all ties and bonds. These aspects all feature in traditional myths and legends. For instance, in her book, *The Jesus of Psychoanalysis* (1979), Dolto argues that the Marriage at Cana, Jesus's first miracle, can be seen as the founding of another home. A young couple pledge their love to one another, breaking the ties with their individual and familiar pasts; a rite takes place in the presence of others, and the wine seals the pact within the community.

The public aspect of marriage underlines the rite's specific nature: the need for testimony and consensus serves to silence the ambivalence that accompanies marriage and, thus, compensate for the attendant loss and mourning. For its psychological aspects, marriage depends on the presence and quantities of identifications within the couple—that is, all the more or less integrated ties and needs, which were contained in past family history and inherited from previous generations. We could, in other words, say that the oedipal structure is constantly repeated, even though each generation restages it with diverse aims, which oscillate between the wish to transform the oedipal scenario and the need to pass it on without making it a subjective psychic event.

Dolto maintains that human beings are born with three desires—maternal, paternal, and infantile. The same could well be said of marriage, when the subject first separates from the mother and, through internalisation of the paternal function, attains the capacity for procreation. But what makes marriage last and what makes it break down? How does a married couple become a parental one?

The duration of marriage is probably linked to the strength of the internal parental couple and their mandate—a mandate that needs to be worked through in order to be transformed. Marriage is also the first step towards reality. Even though it can be undone, because it results from a narcissistic need that cannot be transformed by the couple, due to the massive presence of alienating identifications, marriage is, all the same, an experience that is unconsciously employed to attain some individuation. If, through marriage, the subject has simply attempted to separate from the mother, a degree of internal change has nevertheless been attained.

In his essay on courtship, love, and parenthood, Giannakoulas (1999) argues that the transition from being a couple to being parents is a developmental process which allows the couple to work through the phase of disillusionment from the ecstasies and omnipotence of their initial fusional ideal to establishing mutual trust and sharing various aspects of their lives. This is the necessary developmental achievement to attain the capacity for parenthood—the capacity, in other words, for a triangular relationship. According to Giannakoulas (1999), the triangular relationship goes through its own developmental process; if, initially, the baby is a shared fantasy of the couple (an essential aspect of conception), the parents must work through this fantasy to allow for the real baby to be. Parenthood, he argues, means relinquishing the couple metaphors in order to be in touch with reality.

Freud states that marriage can be an original sort of healing. If the couple complement each other and their needs match, each member is, for the other, the original missing object; in cases in which this does not occur, the marriage breaks up. As he writes in a letter to Ferenczi dated 10 January 1910, separation occurs because the transference cannot be overcome, and, therefore, it goes on being continually displaced (Brabant et al., 1993, pp. 122–124).

The breaking up of a marriage is often an unconscious enactment to defend against the anxiety linked to the perception of the loss of an ideal state. Predominantly, this results from the taking cognisance of an unacceptable reality—in other words, that the other does not meet one's needs. Hence, the wish for reparation underlies the search for a new object to represent and satisfy the inexhaustible search for the original object.

In "On narcissism: an introduction" (1914c), Freud maintains that human beings harbour the unconscious wish to preserve the species. The wish to have a baby meets, first and foremost, a narcissistic need, and a healthy narcissism is essential not only for the continuation of the species, but also for a good enough capacity to care for children. Besides being a feature of our genetic endowment, procreation means repeating what our parents have done. Often, when couples are in crisis, they temporarily hide their difficulties with the fantasy of having a baby, as a way to transform and renew their relationship. However, the concrete experience of procreation cannot make up for the absence of a psychic generative capacity that is part of one's identity. The capacity to generate is entrusted to the body only when it fulfils a narcissistic need linked to a fixation to alienating identifications.

If these alienating identifications are linked to a generational continuity, with no separation, individuation, or capacity to mourn, whatever steps towards reality the subject takes will always be destined to fail. Even parenthood can be part of a narcissistic process that inevitably leads to disappointment, by compulsively repeating the experience of birth, which, for a child, is an inexplicable loss. This is why, when the baby is primarily a fantasised baby, the birth of a child can result in a marital crisis, while the capacity to have a real baby is predicated on the capacity of working through such a fantasy.

In my clinical experience, I have encountered many women who separate from their husbands soon after the birth of a child—often the moment when they unconsciously feel momentarily relieved of their psychopathology. Unconsciously, these women might feel powerful in as much as they displace their own suffering on to the partner, as though the marriage had unconsciously been utilised to give birth to a pathological aspect of the self, which is then abandoned, repressed, or taken care of and repaired outside the self. It is more common, on the other hand, for men to leave their wives when their children reach adolescence, and they find themselves faced with new responsibilities demanding mourning work that has been systematically avoided. Both these clinical occurrences point to the subject functioning mainly along a narcissistic economy, which impoverishes the capacity to acknowledge the other's needs. The lack of real or fantasy recognition is often at the root of an abrupt catastrophe, within both couple and family life. Indeed, when couples split up, there is no capacity to recognise the other, and to acknowledge and meet the other's narcissistic needs.

Angela and Mario both have family histories of serious deprivation, and get married because they are expecting a baby. The marriage is experienced as a mutual taking care of one another, and the birth expected as a miraculous event. Angela comes from a working-class background and, through the marriage, unconsciously wants to make good her humble origins; Mario, who comes from a middle-class family, unconsciously wishes to be helpful and care for someone whom he experiences as part of the self. All throughout the pregnancy, they are attracted to each other's psychopathology, and are like brother and sister playing at being parents by taking care of each other's deprivations.

The real event of the child's birth throws the couple into confusion. He feels abandoned, while she treats the baby like a container of her own anxieties and, at the same time, as an excessive burden. The baby is often sick and the couple becomes increasingly isolated, unable to mourn the loss of the fantasy child that allowed them to conceive. Faced with this predicament, Angela and Mario initially decide to separate and then, postponing this painful decision, come into psychotherapy for help in taking care of their child, who is, by now, two years old. They both bring into the therapy their infantile selves. Feeling contained by the therapy, they become more able to tolerate their child; in some regards, they are like two children sharing a fantasy of having found a good parental model, from which they hope to learn how to be parents. Through the developmental process of the therapy, they are able to move from the narrative of their ideal baby towards a gradual capacity to perceive their child as different from their idealised fantasies.

Angela and Mario do not separate and their relationship with their child improves. They are more able to acknowledge and contain the infant self in one another, and re-experiencing the child self in the relationship with their son proves a source of great joy. Such joy is closely linked to the newfound capacity to feel gratitude for the internal parental couple. Their initial pathological response to the birth of their child was due to their own childhood suffering, which had been split-off and organised as a character defence. I believe that the experience of psychotherapy succeeded in eliciting a positive transference, first of all in relation to their adult self, then in relation to the infantile one.

CHAPTER NINE

Transference: a continuous search for the origin

My reflections stemming from my experience of working with children and adolescents have thus far focused prevalently on their drive to grow and mature, and their identifications. As a therapist, and as a human being, I regard this developmental push as an undoubtedly vital aspect that is firmly oriented towards the future. According to Freud's still very convincing theoretical model, however, our psychic life unfolds simultaneously in two directions which are equally vital, but do not lose sight of the necessity to return to the origin that sooner or later might arise.

In the letter to Ferenczi of 1910, Freud uses "Hans in Luck", a fairy tale by the Brothers Grimm, as a metaphor for the concept of transference (see Appendix). "I want to give you a little piece of theory, which came to me while I was reading your analysis", Freud writes.

> It seems to me that in influencing the sexual drives, we can bring about nothing more than exchanges, displacements; never renunciation, giving up, the resolution of a complex. (Strictest secret!) When someone delivers up his childhood infantile complexes, then in their place he has salvaged a piece of them (the affect) and put it into a present configuration (transference). He has shed his skin and leaves the stripped-off skin for the analyst; God forbid that he is now naked,

skinless! Our therapeutic gain is a substitutive gain, similar to the one Hans im Glück makes. The last piece doesn't fall into the fountain until death. (Brabant et al., 1993, p. 123)

Drawing on this letter, I would argue that transference begins with the original loss, and produces all subsequent economical and dynamic movements of the mind. All psychic operations (such as displacement, condensation, negation, and splitting, or symbolisation and sublimation) are attempts to retrieve the lost object or, at least, to find compensation for the pain of that loss in a way that is compatible with life; conversely, transference represents the unconscious search for that object that has never been reached. I am, therefore, entirely in agreement with Freud's claim in the letter that after many exchanges, the last fragments of transference end only with death.

In developmental movement forward, human beings have no other choice but to continuously exchange objects, so as to hold on to the original object for as long as possible. At the same time, however, the developmental drive pushes the subject to move away from the original object. It is precisely within this theoretical framework that the analytic experience is so important, providing, as it does, the possibility of repeating and decreasing the strength of the bond with the original object, through transformations, displacements, and gradual disinvestments—all emotional investments that are available for new objects. In other words, Freud considered transference to be the force that starts psychic life, and moves it in many directions; in turn, through object exchanges and variations of quantities of drive investments, which never correspond to that original object investment, transference remains at work throughout life, until it comes to an end.

From this perspective, it is clear that the original (i.e., lost) object, in as much as it is rooted in the realm of unconscious phantasies, is a fundamental feature of the subject's imaginary, and is entirely independent of reality. The object-mother is not the original object and cannot substitute it; precisely because it never coincides with the original object, it can never be good enough, even if it is concretely efficient. We could, thus, say, in agreement with Klein, that the object-mother is not just the earliest object, but also the first transference object.

Every clinical experience constitutes a stretch of the route of transference, a slice of life that unfolds according to its own destiny. The experience is always original and unique, even though it develops within a previously ploughed furrow, which will, in turn, provide a trail to follow in later attempts to retrace the developmental steps in search of a different and better adaptation to life. If transference is the unique experience that simultaneously carries and is carried in a certain constructive and developmental direction, proceeding towards a better mental structuring and capacity for object relations, this energy drive must—much like a river—have its own bed to flow in. Indeed, the analyst's containing function is the basic prerequisite for the development of the transference, which is the point of departure for subsequent use of the object in all its gradual and varying complexity.

Mario

Mario is a ten-year-old child in analysis because of intellectual inhibitions. The possibility of facilitating a containing function seemed the most reliable and essential way to keep alive the transference established in our sessions. I was able to provide this containment by functioning as an extension of Mario's self, to which he could entrust his fragmented self, which needed to be held together until the analysis could afford him the developmental help he required. The analysis is, thus, a kind of incubation. Mario's self seems perennially on the brink of fragmenting and dispersing into space, full of an explosive charge that is a by-product of uncontained drive elements. He is less paralysed by the fear of his destructiveness when he establishes the capacity to protect his drive aspects with magical thinking and omnipotence.

About one year into the analysis, Mario invents a game towards the end of a session, which I suggest we might name the "forces of nature". I have the impression that, when our sessions draw to a close, he is compelled to communicate the intense anxiety he is feeling, while, at the same time, needing to tame and keep his drives in check. In the game, Mario acts like a god who has created the universe, gesturing with his hands and uttering guttural sounds that mimic wind, rain, and fire. The howling winds make the door and window slam and everything in the room shake; the rain makes large puddles which Mario slips up in or carefully jumps over; fire invades part of the room, from which we are forced to flee. This game is essential to start thinking.

"Playing", argues Schacht, "creates the relationship while at the same time guaranteeing a comfortable distance" (1988, p. 260, translated for this edition). With Mario, the representation of the drive aspects assumes a dramatic, existential meaning and he personifies and contains them through magical thinking. These omnipotent but illusory dynamics seem to allow him to contain his conflict within the self intermittently, so that he can gradually experience the violence of his drives. In this way, he is able to make contact with aspects of his true self, in the overwhelming emotions he experiences at the end of the session. Mario uses all the objects in the consulting room to represent his drives symbolically by enacting them. Meanwhile, the analyst, in a state of suspension, waits and observes silently so as to become the object created by the patient's transference—that is, the object of his potential true self. The analyst makes herself available to the patient for the transference uses he needs to propose. It is essential that the analyst empty herself of any therapeutic zeal, fantasies, or wishes, with which the patient's false self would comply, repeating his external and internal experience.

In "The destiny drive", Bollas writes, "I think that one of the tasks of an analysis is to enable the analysand to come into contact with his destiny, which means the progressive articulation of his true self through many objects". For Bollas, every object relationship can appear fated when the object imposes a transference movement according to its own unconscious aims or is, instead, the "object through whom the infant establishes and articulates aspects of his destiny" (1989, pp. 45–46).

After the initial outburst of the "forces of nature" game, Mario uses another game to play out the problems he is having at school: he is the teacher in the consulting room–classroom, and I must play the role of the lively and unruly class. The game is repeated over and over again, extensively; I give in easily to his requests to stage it, as I see it as a constructive experience in which he can observe the experiences he has gone through but not worked through.

Out of the blue, Mario's three times weekly analysis is interrupted. The child has the flu; he rings me to tell me he has a temperature and will be unable to come. This is the first time in three years of analysis that we do not meet for a whole week. When he returns he looks lively and vivacious; from the hall, he asks me straight away about our school game: "So have the students been behaving themselves with the supply teacher?" The question reveals a complex transference transformation. Mario shows how aware he is that a separation has taken place, and this awareness is perhaps supported by his realisation that the fragmented aspects of himself can be contained even when he is absent from the session and when his analyst is not there for him. The mention of the supply teacher clearly displays Mario's capacity to envisage the existence of two separate worlds—his own, and the analyst's. Through the capacity to experience the separateness of the two worlds it becomes possible to talk about oneself and ask about the other, to the satisfaction and pleasure of both parties. Whenever we observe the onset of an object relationship, we also notice the strengthening of the ego and its new functions. By asking the question, Mario is also showing his stronger ego, which is more coherent and better integrated and can now make use of displacement, condensation, and symbolisation (as illustrated by his pithy metaphor, which is both complex and ironic). I feel that Mario has found his way of being and can go on developing according to his destiny.

* * *

To let transference find its own expressiveness and reach its full potential is much like a new life finding embodiment so that the body can realise its own destiny—to be oneself in relation to the world, and take responsibility for that relationship. The child's transference is not addressed to a particular object in the world, because she has not defined her objects yet. Her affects aim towards the whole of her surroundings—to a world that is yet to be discovered, which her investments will draw on. There is always something new emerging from transference, which leads us to conclude that the aspect of repetition is the less significant, secondary feature of the phenomenon—a faint echo of the past, which confers coherence and continuity to the subject's narration. It is the constructive and non-repetitive aspects of the present moment that, in their novelty and actuality, provide new experiences which increment previous ones, while also interacting and adapting to the latter, so as to guarantee stability and consolidation of the lived past. These new experiences are creations of the analytic relationship and give meaning to the process of psychic transformations. The present is built by re-signifying the past. Experiences are enriched through the continuous flow of projections and introjections, even if repetition seems to defy the passage of time, addressing the past—recent or remote—as if it could be grafted on the original experience in a seemingly undifferentiated manner. Yet, it is precisely in this very dynamic that the original experience is gradually transformed.

If transference means that the affects of childhood object ties are always repeated with new objects encountered through the course of life, with child patients we can see how the foundations for the transference are laid—we can, as it were, see transference "en route".

Pietro (whose return to analysis I mentioned in Chapter Six, and will return to in Chapter Ten) is a three-year-old boy who shows autistic traits. In all his symbolic play, behaviour, and gestures in our sessions, he lists the things he has come across before the session that have affected him positively or negatively. Analysis is the chosen environment for the transfer of current emotions into a symbolic register, a way of building interconnected, structured narrations from unstable, variable events.

Analytic work takes place not only through interpretations, but also through the representation of things as they come up in the relationship. For example, when Pietro cries in our first session, my intervention—drawing a picture of the child with his father—seeks to go beyond the verbal and, thus, to stimulate it. Pietro comes into contact with me after being dropped off at my consulting room by his father; mine is, therefore, a depiction of the relational environment that has just been lost. Similarly, when Pietro does not speak, I draw a map of the walk from the child's house to my consulting room, dwelling particularly on the square halfway between the two as a point of encounter and transition. Rather than interpreting or spelling out the child's needs or the content of his suffering (which his ego would not easily have tolerated), the analytic work centred on representing things, which are the foundation of symbolic processes and the subject's ability to interact with the world in order to introject it.

One day, Pietro introduces a new element in his play, mapping out the "town of Anghiari"—the town his paternal grandparents come from, where he usually spends his holidays. I find the way in which this occurs and develops particularly interesting. Initially, Pietro chooses to reconstruct his version of this town in a darkened corner of the room, separate from the area in front of the window where he usually plays. It seems that staging his representation in the dark is so important to Pietro that not only does he set up this imagined town behind a chest of drawers, as if to shield himself from view, but also closes the shutters in the consulting room, leaving us in semi-darkness.

With his game, Pietro seems to be attempting to transfer into the analysis and represent the original core of the self, which he doggedly protects and defends against external stimuli. This original core he is drawing on evidently enclosed the experiences of several generations. Apparently, the barely structured mind of the child was capable of forming a transference that contained the wish to restore a prior condition, which had not yet been transformed—by the passage of time, and through displacement and condensation—into his personal history, but that he felt he had lived briefly and then lost. When early experiences have not been placed in historical time, they inform the present by signifying a fleetingly known experience, which has not yet been worked through and, consequently, inserted in a wider spatio-temporal dimension. Thus, the child homogenises and juxtaposes both past and present relational contexts, rather than differentiating them as an adult mind would.

Collapsing history and prehistory into the same spatio-temporal context, as though it were a continuous immanent experience, is a form the child's mind takes, and the child always refers to time as "before". Relating every experience back to that origin is a way of expanding and getting to know affective and cognitive experiences, and, thereby, reinforcing the subjective sense of continuity and owner-ship. The fundamental aspects for the construction of the internal world and, therefore, of one's identity are closely dependent on rela-tionships, the dynamics and meanings of which are represented in the transference. Superimposing different experiences as if they were the same increases the intensity of the experience, prepares and initi-ates the formation of displacement and condensation, and gives depth and complexity to the transition between primary and secondary process functioning.

To better comprehend the phenomenon of dreams, Freud (1900a) understands the concept of transference as a movement between different levels of the psychic topography and a movement of the unconscious drives towards conscious representation. For this dyna-mic movement to be possible, it is necessary that drives be closely linked with day residues (i.e., with the subject's representations of his present relationships). Through condensation, the day residues acquire the meaning of emotional and cognitive experiences and the drive can legitimately be represented in the conscious mind. This twofold function carries within it the "dual vectors" of the transference.

Transference is, therefore, not only the tendency to make good a lack or a loss, but also a fundamental effort to build, broaden, and enrich knowledge of the self and the world, while continuing to aim unconsciously to fill an absence or repair a loss. In short, transference is the movement of the drive force that replenishes itself with the resources of its origin. And as it concerns the transformation and organisation of the mind's primitive chaos, it is, therefore, necessary that the primitive and chaotic drive energy—which has not yet found objects that can substitute the original object—find containment and direction.

If we conceptualise transference as a return to the origin, the function of the analyst does not only consist in recognising the transference, but also in eliciting and organising it. Through the experience that the self has in the transference relationship, the ego acquires new capacities and functions. The transference communication is not necessarily addressed to a particular object or person, but can attach itself to anything. Within a relational conceptualisation, transference can be seen as a way of getting to know the world.

Pietro's invention of the town of Anghiari is his way of returning to the origin, a return made necessary by the intense pain he experienced when his sister was born. With the acceptance of psychic pain comes the need to return to one's origin, and to question one's origin is also to be curious about one's birth. This is why Pietro needs to repeat his journey to Anghiari in the transference. But going to Anghiari is also the only sign of the newfound possibility of mourning the loss and reinvesting life—an indication of the aliveness of the transference.

To explain transference's dual vector, it is useful to revisit the two meanings that Freud gives to the concept of transference, in dream and clinical work. In child analysis, the first meaning of transference refers to the work carried out by the child to give meaning to his experiences, drawing on the day residues to better understand the self. In the second sense, transference traces an itinerary, shared by both child and analyst, leading to a return to the origin.

Freud uses the fairy tale of "Hans in Luck" (see Appendix) as a metaphor to suggest that, throughout life, transference is interminable. Like Hans collecting and exchanging objects in the story, the subject is able to advance in acquiring self-knowledge and a sense of identity only through continuous displacements onto different objects and relationships with which to identify. Identity is, therefore, never definitive, but always reorganised in relation to the experiences and relationships that we live in any one moment. Corollary to this, of course, is the question of whether psychotherapy might be terminable or interminable.

CHAPTER TEN

On analysis terminable and interminable

F reud's essay "Analysis terminable and interminable" (1937c) occupies an important place in his legacy. In this text, he represents psychic functioning as hinging on a twofold temporal and atemporal dimension. In the temporal dimension of secondary functioning, it is very difficult to include and address the timelessness of the unconscious, in which analysis is interminable.

Surveying the psychoanalytic literature, one encounters two major theories regarding the conclusion of analysis, which rely closely on different theoretical frameworks. One theory puts the emphasis on psychotherapeutic results and the importance of short-term treatment, especially when patients are children or adolescents and therapy can help them get back on a developmental track to face life changes. (At times this thinking is also applied to more disturbed patients.) The other perspective advocates lengthier analysis and harbours different views on recovery.

There is, in fact, no real opposition between these two perspectives. It is important for the analyst not to hold on to her patients, and that treatment should, thus, be terminable, but it is also true that analysis *per se* is interminable and goes on even in the post-treatment phases. As long as there is an unconscious mind, there is space for symptom formation, even if these symptoms change, improve, or give way to others. The difference between therapy and analysis is that there is potentially unlimited scope for the analysis of unconscious derivatives, while therapy is the employment of this method compatible with the necessary aim of symptom relief and negotiation with reality. I would also add that various factors contribute to bringing about the conclusion of treatment, which can be determined by the patient, parents, or therapist. This cannot, however, be defined as the end of the analysis.

During analysis, the patient has the experience of timelessness. Who, then, decides when it is time to end? Usually, conscious criteria are used to decide termination, but the analytic relationship also includes a deeper, unconscious level, occurring almost in a parallel realm (of which *Alice through the Looking Glass* could be an apt metaphor). In this sense, the analytic relationship resembles an interminable dimension: it is only for economic reasons, both psychological and concrete, that we must introduce the possibility of termination. The actual length of analytic treatment reintroduces real time; analysis in itself has no duration, as it exists outside time.

Introducing chronological time into the interminability of analysis gives the possibility of conclusion. Much as it is difficult to acknowledge, termination is almost always brought about by external reasons with which therapists must abide. Sometimes, parents want their child or adolescent to remain in the therapy, fearing a relapse, which they hope to prevent by continuing treatment. Sometimes, the child or adolescent has difficulty parting, having replaced the protection given by the family with that provided by the therapy.

Especially in the treatment of very disturbed patients, the analyst can find himself in the difficult position of being afraid of not having done enough to help, while, at the same time, desiring to be free of the patient. In navigating between the Scylla of guilt or responsibility and the Charybdis of suffering, the analyst tries to find a safe route to termination. Of course, this all occurs within the dimension of the unconscious relationship; these matters cannot be expressed as such and, therefore, need to find conscious justifications that are coherent with the sense of reality.

Every human being has passively experienced trauma, which they actively re-enact. And every patient comes to analysis with a burden of traumata, experienced and caused. But what can analysis do in relation to this trauma? I do not think the question is simply one of working through the trauma; rather, I believe analysis can permit the subject to put to different uses the investments employed to encapsulate the trauma, so as to be able to use these, together with aspects of the trauma itself, in the construction of self. I shall relate, here, a case of a very painful termination, which proved difficult for both patient and analyst.

Anna is a thirty-year-old woman, in analysis for severe depression. After ten years in which the very idea of finishing seemed inconceivable, she feels more secure within herself and expresses the need to conclude the therapy. She is very emotional but appears resolute. In recent years, she has begun to take pleasure in caring for her family, even doing some volunteer work on the side. In our last session, she brings a dream, in which she returned to her childhood home, only to find a "to let" sign on the door. She asked the janitor of the building to allow her to see her childhood home one more time.

Anna's narration of the dream brings to mind that a teenage boy once rang my doorbell to ask if I would let him in to take a look at my garden, in which he remembered planting a fig tree when he was little. After seeing the tree, the boy left, content, and it seemed to me that Anna was now able to do something similar. She no longer harboured any resentment towards her parents—feelings that had prevented her from ever speaking fondly about her early childhood—and at long last could think of them with affection and pleasure. Anna's case embodies what Bruno Schulz terms "matur[ing] into childhood" (1990, p. 26).

But when is the time right for the patient to feel able to leave therapy? During the process of mourning, Freud claims that investments are withdrawn from the lost object and then reinvested on other objects, indicating that the underlying work is the work of displacement. And in the aforementioned letter to Ferenczi of 1910 (seven years before "Mourning and melancholia"), Freud talks about the tenacity of transference, in its constant displacement onto other objects. As seen in the previous chapter, Freud uses "Hans in Luck" as an analogy for transference passing from one object to another and terminating only with death.

*   *   *

Thinking back on my child patients, as I often do, I notice that some disappear as soon as their symptoms do. If we see these symptoms as a desperate way of communicating their needs and attracting attention, perhaps the exact same thing happens when they leave, replacing their symptoms with exchanges and relationships within the fabric of their family life.

It is common to attribute the sudden decision to conclude treatment to the resistance of the parents (or, at least, the dominant one) and their difficulties tolerating a deepening of the therapy. If the parents have unconsciously designated their child to carry psychopathology, this is probably determined by the child's equally pathological need to cure the parents, to his own detriment. We might also wonder whether a decision to conclude treatment that is apparently taken by the parents might also, in fact, belong to the child and the analyst, and be a compromise formation between the individual needs of the child and his needs to repair the parents (which concerns child and therapist alike). Indeed, since it is invariably the parents who request that their child enter therapy, thus expressing the child's needs along with their own, an important aspect of the therapist's aims might be the reparation of the infantile self, to no longer disappoint parental expectations. In this sense, therapist and child are allies in their developmental endeavour: indeed, the work of reparation relies on the therapist's availability to be repaired, so as to facilitate the transformation of the internal objects that were damaged and, therefore, are not available as objects for identification.

I believe that we may address the issue of termination from both a theoretical and an ideological point of view. If the analyst sees the child–parent relationship as rivalrous and, therefore, potentially destructive, she must necessarily interpret the whole context as pathological and, consequently, adopt a competitive stance in relation to the family system. Alternatively, if the analyst sees in the child–parent relationship an essentially vital core, one that struggles to survive because it is burdened by trauma, but where the trauma is not necessarily caused by the actors on the scene (since the traumatic condition might be the best they can muster given the internal and external conditions), then she will interpret that vital core as something to defend and reinforce, so as to enhance its capacity to work through the traumas which make up its core. It is not easy to discern which of these theoretical positions is more scientifically feasible, and, given that the analyst is also motivated by personal values and sets of beliefs, I would contend that the analyst's stance contains an ideological aspect, which, in turn, can represent a displacement or condensation of her own repressed affects or traumata. In sum, I do not think that, in practice, one position is more tenable than the other, but have the impression that they oscillate or alternate within the same psychotherapy.

Manzano and colleagues concisely define the parental predicament as "the mourning of development" (2001, p. 16, translated for this edition), part of the process of transformation that human beings go through, from the gradual renunciation of their infantile condition to the progressive acquisition of a parental function. In other words, the capacity for parenthood is closely linked to the capacity to tolerate the loss of the object. And as mourning is an interminable process for all human beings, the analyst also experiences the same vicissitudes; indeed, when intervening in the child–parent relationship, analysts should always ask themselves whether they instinctively side with child or parent.

When, years later, I think back on the endings of child therapies, I am often struck by an aspect that at the time I failed to take fully into account. A child in analysis is always exposed to a trauma or multiple traumas, whether recent or past, and the child and parent alike ask for help to heal these open wounds, which engender anxiety. They need to be helped to forget rather than to remember; however, for the wound to heal properly, it must be reopened. This process does not occur in a linear way, but, rather, oscillates continuously between attempts to examine more deeply and efforts to provide temporary cover. If, for example, the analyst detects intolerable suffering (related, let us say, to the child's oral dependency, which can contain intense mutual aggression), she will almost certainly see that the child's play will display the identification with the object whom he depends on— and this will magically alleviate this suffering. In this case, the analyst does not need to interpret, because she knows that the child is, thus, commencing a healing process. Of course, even the most primitive defences from pain have omnipotent and magical characteristics, but are the inevitable starting point from which more complex and sophisticated constructions can begin.

To define child psychotherapy in essential terms, we could say that it consists in facilitating the repression of the trauma and the attendant opening up of the ego to the possibility of constructing subjective identity on a more secure base. The conclusion of child analysis is, thus, a way of putting development back on track, or at least setting it on a more secure path. Consequently, analysis can end when the child, therapist, and parents have had an experience of internal reconciliation—a lessening of the conflict between infantile aspects and fragile pseudo-adult ones.

The end of child analysis, to sum up, is not reached because everything has been worked through; it could, in fact, be seen as a necessary latency period that helps the child work through and silently introject the experience of the analytic relationship. To better illustrate these points, I will share my reflections on a child whom I saw for four years of psychotherapy, from age three to seven (see Chapter Nine), and who resumed work in adolescence.

Pietro's return

The adolescent returning to analysis after a successful therapy that has receded into a latency state finds himself in a peculiar position. As the analysis led to the capacity to repress, the therapy itself has been repressed, too. Hence, when the adolescent resumes analytic work, he does not willingly pick up where he left off, but, rather, desires a new experience. Having repressed the oedipal conflicts, he revisits those same conflicts differently during adolescence (essentially through displacements and splittings into good and bad object), without linking the present with his memory of them. The adolescent suffers, but does not know why.

The event of a return to analysis raises important questions. Should the analyst avoid touching on what has been repressed? Or should she try instead to re-evoke this repressed childhood? She has, after all, been part of the process, and still remembers the consulting room packed with the child's toys.

In cases like these, I do not think that the analyst's main task is to encourage the return of the repressed. This is partly because repression is a necessary condition for separation, and, consequently, patient and analyst each have an individual and subjective representation of the repressed content. This content must be discovered anew, and we must, therefore, assume that the patient who returns is a different patient.

It is natural to wonder why one child might return, while another does not. In my experience, adolescents who return still have some mourning work to do, and, consequently, summon the courage to face their internal objects again in a context of decreased dependency. I think this occurs especially with regard to aggressive aspects, which, in the context of extreme dependency, often cannot be expressed. Pietro's return, for example, was motivated by strong aggressiveness toward his objects and self.

I must, first of all, confess that seeing a young patient again after many years (particularly when the analyst–patient relationship was profound, and the young child one knew returns as an adolescent) is a deeply emotional and strongly ambivalent experience. In terms of the ever-present feeling of omnipotence, the return can be seen as a failure; on the other hand, however, it affords an almost narcissistic pleasure, as if the patient could not do without us.

After his sixteenth birthday, Pietro phones me to ask if he can return to therapy, as he is going through a distressing spell. Our meeting is emotional for both of us, and the analytic setting, established all those years ago, helps us to measure ourselves against one another. Pietro has a strong desire to be listened to, and speaks continuously without letting me get a word in edgeways—I also sense he is afraid I might make a reference to the past. The main reason for his coming back to see me is a romantic disappointment that has left him feeling disorientated and lost. He says he remembers very little of our previous analysis, and that the years following it were not easy for him.

Seven years after terminating, he met a twelve-year-old girl—a classmate of his sister's—with whom he established a loving friendship and to whom he grew very attached. The relationship lasted about a year, after which the girl, who is two years younger than him, began to be increasingly distant, making excuses not to see him. Not knowing how to explain her behaviour, she attributed the blame to his being older, and her family's opposition to the bond. Pietro felt completely lost in dealing with this situation. Separating from his difficult family environment had been a slow and painful process; now, after the breakup, he sinks back into the familial context, asking his mother to be his confidante and defend his failures, even threatening to commit suicide if she does not. In this state of depression and malaise, he turns to me for help.

In the first sessions, he speaks obsessively about his relationship with the girl and asks me if he can draw a picture—something he is very good at, and a strong relational mode of his childhood therapy.

He sketches out large faces that look a lot like his, and smiles, pleased with his abilities. He signs the pictures emphatically, with a big, flourishing signature.

Pietro seems to need to re-encounter the analyst in person to validate his achieved sense of identity. This is, I suspect, only an official or incomplete version of his identity, as in another drawing he represents his state as a prison. The image and story of his breakup seem to relate, albeit in a different way, to the trauma that first brought Pietro into analysis when he was three—the birth of his sister, a very traumatic event for him. This trauma had not been fully grasped by his family and had even led him to adopt an autistic muteness. In his current situation, there was certainly displacement at work—in place of his sister there was his sister's friend, and an image condensing the figures of the mother, sister, and her friend represented the lost object and ensuing pain.

There was, however, an altogether new element in this representation—anger had taken the place of mute withdrawal, and Pietro displayed a psychotic refusal of reality. In his drawings, Pietro depicted reality as a prison, and his feelings oscillate between two all-encompassing visions: acceptance of the prison as an extreme form of containment on the one hand; rebellion and total destruction, on the other. This also signals that he has not renounced his oedipal complex.

An attempt to renounce the oedipal struggle takes place in the latency stage, but, in adolescence, the conflict resurfaces with great force and virulence with the reawakening of the drives. This reawakening is often experienced as a need for revenge or a form of compensation for trauma. Very often, in narcissistic family constellations such as Pietro's, the child must suffer the trauma of narcissistic violence and cannot engage in oedipal rivalry, because he is not recognised as an object. He is left with no object to love but filled, instead, with omnipotent hatred as he enters adolescence, when he strives to become potent or at least be recognised as a subject. Hatred, therefore, is an important tool that can permit a narcissistic family constellation with no proper relationships to change, and push it in the direction of object relations.

After resuming therapy, Pietro frequently expresses his hatred, both in our sessions and at home. At times he feels so much hatred that he voices the wish to direct it against himself. He then gradually begins to intuit what links the material that he brings into the sessions.

The possibility of experiencing his anger and expressing it in a containing situation is such a relief for him that it makes my effort to contain it feel worthwhile. In her essay "The adolescent novel" (1993), Kristeva argues that adolescence is a recapitulation of the modes of being that were learnt in childhood. It seems to me that Pietro is using this opportunity to bring back states of mind that relate to his origin.

Pietro starts bringing photographs of his family to our sessions. He shows them to me and uses them to communicate—with words, rather than through play, as he used to—about his origins, the comics he draws with his friends, the trips they go on, the slang they speak. Pietro also talks about his love of cinema, showing a surprising level of expertise. I entertain the fantasy that perhaps I had somehow communicated my own passion for cinema to him—an irrational thought, of course, as I had never mentioned it.

Pietro's communications seem gradually to weave a degree of continuity between his childhood situation and his current, teenage one. He does not want me to substitute for the missing object, and is, instead, working to construct or re-find the internal bond with the object. The question, however, remains: why had he returned to therapy? What did he really want from me? A year passes, and, in one of our final sessions, he says that he remembers little of his childhood; among the few things he does recall, he knows he came round to play with me, and saw me as a sort of aunt. The few faded memories he has of this are positive.

I suspect that Pietro had returned to therapy to work through the loss of the previous therapeutic experience—something that, at the time, he had been unable to do, and still needed to be done—because I represented the transference knot separating him from his father, a knot he wanted to untie without being overcome with guilt. This resembles the oedipal solution through displacement that had emerged in a later phase of his child analysis ("Let's pretend that we are husband and wife", he once told me, "and that Mummy is Grandma"), following the articulation of another fantasy: "Let's pretend Daddy is dead and that Mummy marries a little boy-stepsister".

Only after rereading a paper I had written some years before did I become aware of an odd coincidence: Pietro's sentimental attachment to his sister's friend had lasted one year, and the same time had elapsed between the resumption of his analysis and its end. After a year he had decided to "leave" me—perhaps this was his way of feeling compensated.

This hypothesis would also suggest that Pietro had managed to reorganise his defences in such a way that could afford the experience of loss, without this entailing a mutilation of his identity. Indeed, it seems to me that Pietro left the therapy feeling enriched by his own potential and much more self-confident. After all, it is only with the capacity to experience loss—or to find a substitute or displacement object, as discussed in the previous chapter on transference—that the subject can gradually separate and individuate, and construct his identity.

CHAPTER ELEVEN

Loss and its destinies

> As I kneel at the graves, I am often met
> With a great vision of fate; and for a moment
> Destiny appears, like a firmament
> Where in place of stars I see souls.
>
> (Hugo, "Les Malheureux", 1856, p. 326, translated for this edition)

The question of loss shares its origins with the birth of human-ity itself. In the Bible, Adam and Eve are expelled from paradise and condemned to earn their bread by daily toil, all earthly life originating from a loss. In our culture, we have moved from biblical tradition to individual myth, in which the child who is born loses the union with the mother.

Psychoanalysis proposes that loss is an occurrence repeated throughout infancy: weaning, toilet training, dentition, the first steps, and the first words, these all represent ways to articulate loss, as the child gradually grows and moves away from the beginnings of life. Mourning is one of the psychic modes through which human beings are transformed after a loss.

Freud addresses the subject of loss extensively in "Mourning and melancholia". He writes,

> Mourning is regularly the reaction to the loss of a loved person, or to the loss of some abstraction which has taken the place of one, such as one's country, liberty, an ideal and so on. In some people the same influences produce melancholia instead of mourning and we consequently suspect them of a pathological disposition. (1917e, p. 243)

The difference between mourning and melancholia, thus, would be accounted for by the object choice: the former is related to anaclitic object choice, the latter follows a narcissistic one. While in mourning, the object cathexes are detached from the lost object and displaced to new ones to go on living; in melancholia, the loss cannot be overcome: "The shadow of the object fell upon the ego" (1917e, p. 249).

For the melancholic, loss seems to belong to the feelings linked with the death drive, while the work of mourning signals that Eros is engaged in having the upper hand on the lost object. In melancholia, the shadow of the object falls upon a rudimentary ego, which has yet to build itself as its own drive patrimony, and, thus, cannot mourn something it lacks. In this sense, the shadow of the object has to be understood as the negative of the object's cathexes on the subject; the latter, whose reservoir of libido is still poor, has, as sole vital resources, those coming from the object.

Loss is always an experience of the limit. When it occurs, it takes our breath away, as if we, too, are going to die with the lost object. When we are able to breathe again, though, we know that the air belongs to us, that we have survived. To survive loss means carrying a trauma inside oneself, which isolates the painful core of loss without working it through. It is, therefore, fated to be renewed continuously and in all sorts of forms, albeit dulled by isolation.

Perhaps, as Freud claims, the melancholic subject is overshadowed by the object and tyrannised by a cruel superego, and we may, thus, speak of a loss of self. The problem, when treating a melancholic subject, is the incapacity to work through and symbolise. He rages against the visibility of the work, which is, thus, constantly obscured; his body does not offer itself, for fear of encountering an absent gaze. Required to find a meaning precisely where it is negated, the analyst holds on to the body that comes to the session and communicates its presence, and can only legitimate that bodily presence devoid of any apparent meaning. The noumenon of the melancholic's body resides in the need of the one who conceived it; anonymity and meaninglessness, paradoxically, give the melancholic the power to be there, thanks to the therapist's legitimation.

Those who seek analysis hope it might provide an opportunity for restitution of past losses, which can be expressed on both the concrete and the symbolic levels. What is at stake is, at times, not the loss, but the denunciation of a lack; transposed to the present context, this aims simultaneously to claim possession of the object along with its eventual loss, thus legitimising the demanded restitution through a displacement. Of course, to denounce a loss regards a presumption of possession. I would add, the loss of a love, frequently encountered in analysis, is the loss of a completeness that is synonymous with an original wholeness. This is represented very well, for example, in the myth of the androgyne told by Aristophanes in Plato's *Symposium* (2008).

According to Klein, the subject who, in childhood, has worked through the depressive position is better equipped to face life's mournful experiences. In "Mourning and its relation to manic-depressive states" (2017[1940]), she writes, "My contention is that the child goes through states of mind comparable to the mourning of the adult, or rather, that this early mourning is revived whenever grief is experienced in later life" (2017, p. 344). The loss of the breast, which the child experiences as a consequence of his greed, is an emblem of all future loss. "In short—persecution (by 'bad' objects) and the characteristic defences against it, on the one hand, and pining for the loved ('good') object, on the other, constitute the depressive position" (2017, p. 348).

Each time the adult suffers a loss, he re-experiences the original infantile depression. It is, consequently, very important to understand how the child negotiated the depressive position; if he has been able to work through it, and, thus, become separate from the object, when he suffers further losses these are not experienced as a loss of the self. (This does not concern the loss of important object relationships, which always at least partially entail a quota of narcissistic investment.)

As far as childhood is concerned, the onset of time and space creates a tragic dimension. The acceleration of time results in the loss of infantile helplessness. The child seems to reach out and conquer a greater autonomy, as Ferenczi remarks, with some irony, in "The dream of the clever baby": "The wish to become great and to excel over 'the great' in wisdom and knowledge is only a reversal of the contrary situation of the child" (1980, pp. 349–350).

The dream of the clever baby related by Ferenczi probably expresses the adult patient's fear of reliving the state of infantile helplessness in the analysis, a state felt to be tantamount to madness and fear of loss of identity. In fact, the experience of loss leads the subject to re-experience what Winnicott calls the "unthinkable anxiety"—that is, that the mother might leave and the infant be too young to be able to hold her in mind. This is especially true when the child experiences loss passively, and is not yet able to foresee it. By contrast, when the baby has already internalised the mother in her presence and absence (as Freud observes, in *Beyond the Pleasure Principle* (1920g), in relation to his grandson), the absence of the mother is represented metaphorically through the "fort–da" game. The child's ability to play this game signals an ability to symbolise events and experience them as the effect of individual actions.

In her article "About losing and being lost" (1967), Anna Freud discusses symbolisation. She considers Winnicott's concept of the "transitional object", which allows a gradual transition from the breast to the thumb to "the blanket, pillow, or soft, cuddly toy which is played with" (1967, p. 11). These primary objects are invested both narcissistically and with object love, and constitute the passage from love for the mother to interest in the world. Both animate and inanimate objects represent the original object on which children and adults project their anger, sadness, and affects. These displacements are experienced as plausible substitutes for the object or, at least, some of its aspects, while the compulsive, fetishistic search for objects (like that, for example, of collectors) reveals how, ultimately, all objects are unable to stand in for the original object. Investment and disinvestment, especially on material objects, is a constant throughout our lives, thus loss is a part of the daily oscillations that positively or negatively affect our moods.

The loss of a very intense investment (like an important love) is altogether different, as it deeply undermines a person's stability. In his essay *Perdre de vue* [*Losing from sight*], Pontalis (1988) focuses on the question of seeing and no longer seeing the love object. He relates a painful conversation between a man, who has lost his mother, and his close friend. After his mother's death, the man says, he will no longer be able to see her, and—crucially—will no longer be seen by her. The subject who is no longer the object of the other's gaze no longer feels his own existence, as there is no object to confirm it—and it is even possible to doubt whether he has ever been the object of the maternal gaze (see Winnicott, "Mirror-role of mother and family in child development", 2005b).

The importance of the gaze in the relationship with the object intensifies when the object has not been introjected, hence the need to hold onto it and to be held in sight. Beside other aspects, the need to control the object leads to a form of repetition compulsion that is very difficult to work through. As Pontalis writes: "It is necessary that the image, in its overshadowing presence, is erased and at the same time remains in its absence. The invisible is not the negation of what is visible: it is in it, inhabits it, and is its horizon and beginning. When the loss is *in* sight, it ceases to be an interminable mourning" (1988, p. 325, translated for this edition).

Returning to the aforementioned essay, Anna Freud places emphasis not simply on the loss *per se*, but also on the identification with the lost object of the person who loses something. In this light, we can see the importance of Klein's projective identification with the objects, and the impact they can have on suffering and the sense of lack. Another of Anna Freud's insightful observations regards the significance of the experience of being lost. When children are lost to their parents' gaze and loving mindfulness, they lose themselves. To lose and be lost signals the traumatic experiences that we often intuit in the narratives of adult patients who seek analysis, although these are seldom events they themselves remember, but have been told about by their parents when they were older.

A patient with fantasies of having never been loved by her mother (who seemed to prefer her elder son) tells me about a memory that is very painful and traumatic, and which she is unsure is fully hers. Five years old at the time, she was out with her parents and had asked them to buy her an ice cream. When they refused, she had walked off alone, and her parents had not followed her. On her way home, she had got lost and was hit by a car while crossing the road. The impact had nearly killed her and she had spent a long spell in hospital in great pain. During this time, she remembers her father had seemed very emotionally close.

Anna Freud writes,

> It is only when parental feelings are ineffective or too ambivalent, or when their aggression is more effective than their love, or when the mother's emotions are temporarily engaged elsewhere, that children not only feel lost but, in fact, get lost. (1967, pp. 15–16)

Another patient, who endured a painfully lonely childhood, also relates childhood recollections of getting lost. Many years later, she publishes a book of poems, and writes in my copy, "To the person who led me here".

What, then, is the fate of loss in analysis? How best to fill the void of thoughts and representations? Very often, patients seek therapy because they have lost someone or something, be it a child, a parent, a love object, their possessions, or their job. What transformational work can be performed in analysis? How do we deal with loss, and how do we work through it? Some mourning work is undoubtedly possible, and is often done to build up defences; I wonder, however, whether the work of mourning can ever be terminated or is, indeed, terminable.

In Chapter Two, I described my clinical work with Silvia, a child who relives her infantile trauma retrospectively (*nachträglich*) at the onset of puberty (Gutton, 1991). Silvia works through her experience of loss as she is negotiating this new developmental step—this suggests that it is, indeed, possible for childhood experiences to be given a new meaning, and, therefore, a new psychic function.

While the factors that constitute identity draw on their transgenerational and generational origins, the work of identity takes place through the life events through which we articulate our destiny and which shake our initial identity structure with varying degrees of intensity. My personal and professional identity, for example, was deeply affected by the loss of my only daughter. It is often said that losing a child is an unnatural, even inhuman, event, because parents should die before their children. The experience brings unspeakable pain, and it is probably impossible ever to completely work through. Thankfully, at the time, I could rely on strong support and had many patients to treat; indeed, I think that my work became a source of tentative reparation, a way of continuing to care for my daughter through all my patients. The sudden loss of a daughter destroys all sense of the future, makes us feel irreparably broken. We lose integrity, wholeness, the illusion of having control over the world, and the joy of beholding someone who brightens our life and resembles us. The event inflicted a grave loss to the omnipotence present in all aspects of life. Every gesture is relived and lost; every word or action that is recalled will disappear. Who knows if words can ever fully convey such unrelenting pain, which engulfs every aspect of life, imbues the whole world, and makes one feel as if one no longer exists?

Words convey emotions and thoughts, translate dreams; even writing these lines allows me to speak to all those who have felt the same grief, to those who have seen it reflected in others. Now, many years later, I can see that taking care of my patients allowed me to carry on living; thanks to them (as Winnicott says, dedicating *Playing and Reality* to his patients) and a continuous self-analysis, I was able to alleviate my sense of loss and the difficulties of working it through.

Poets have often turned to their art to attempt to work through terrible losses. Victor Hugo, for example, dedicated one of his most beautiful poems to his daughter Léopoldine, after she drowned in the Seine near Villequier. It was 1843, and his daughter was nineteen. The internal experience of loss and its working through is eloquently expressed in these lines taken from his collection, *Les Contemplations*.

> Tomorrow, at dawn, when the fields are pale,
> I'll leave. You see, I know that you await me.
> I'll cross the forest, and cross the mountain.
> No longer can I be without you.
>
> I'll walk with eyes fixed on my thoughts,
> Seeing nothing around me, hearing no noise,
> Alone, unknown, back bent, hands crossed,
> Day for me will be like night.
>
> I'll see neither the gold of falling evening,
> Nor the distant sails en route to Harfleur,
> And when I arrive, I'll place on your tomb
> A bouquet of holly and heather in bloom
> (1856, p. 253, translated for this edition)

The experience of loss always has a base in reality, whatever the lost object or its value might be for the subject. It follows that, if the subject feels unable to bear the pain of the losses that reality inevitably inflicts on human beings, one possible strategy is to replace the lost object. When the need to remain faithful to the lost object is strong, however, every attempt to find a suitable substitute is doomed to fail. In this case, the only other feasible form of compensation, besides melancholia, is a shared delusional ritual—putting flowers on the grave, observing religious rites, demanding collective participation to personal grief, believing in and seeking magical and supernatural communication.

I hold that the most constructive and life-enhancing form of mourning loss is transference. As suggested above, the work of identity unfolds through transference: it is transference that gives us the possibility of exiting our narcissistic enclosure to encounter the objects of our desire. We come into contact with these objects throughout our whole life, just as in the aforementioned fairy tale of "Hans in Luck" (see Chapter Nine and Appendix). Of course, as is the case for Hans, the power and value of these objects diminish as we grow older, but, in any case, they endure over time. This is why, in the story, Hans thanks his Master and feels fortunate—life is so full of possibility and our imagination so very fertile.

When the loss is too great, however, I believe that the subject in mourning does not really benefit from making a displacement onto a different object—rather, I would argue that the most life-enhancing and responsible form of reparation in these cases is identifying with the lost object. It is undeniable, all the same, that depressive affects are involved, due to the absence of the body of the object and the lack of future developments, which the subject has to come to terms with psychically. The process of identification concerns a profound working through of the past relationship with the lost object, which inevitably results in giving new meanings to all the mutual attributions. Ultimately, it is a movement whereby both the self and the lost object find new identifications.

CHAPTER TWELVE

Treating psychotic children: the experience of anonymity or the feeling of losing one's identity

P sychoanalytic work continuously challenges the psychotherapist's identity. Her sense of self must have a solid core, in order
for her to be available and reliable for her patients, but must
also be sufficiently flexible, so that it can be transformed and adapted
in the encounter with patients who need to feel that they can fashion
their objects. It is particularly trying to be the therapist of a psychotic
patient—almost as if the analyst needs constantly to make up a new
identity, to maintain a space for observation beyond the confusion.

Individuals who are in the throes of a strong reality since the
beginning of their psychic life do not believe that such reality can be
turned into their history. They find it unthinkable that this would not
leave a gaping hole, attracting every subsequent event, which would
simply configure itself as an endless and sterile repetition of that original happening.

In *The Violence of Interpretation* (2001), Aulagnier proposes that the
psychotic is someone who cannot think of a function independently
from the characters who have been its first representatives and are
destined forever to remain such. The psychotic, she argues, cannot
think of herself as a child, but only as the child of a particular couple.
"The universal is annulled in a particular, accidental element", writes

Aulagnier. "The concept loses all universal meaning and, by the same token, any ability to symbolise; it becomes a prisoner of the physical thing that embodies it" (2001, p. 122). This reminds me a little of the passage cited from Bernhard's memoir in Chapter Seven. Just as in a Shakespearian tragedy, all elements are present from the beginning, and what happens at the end takes place due to unavoidable fate, the consequence of an unforeseeable clot of reality.

"When a psychic and relational process is characterised by the lacuna of its origins or its dramatic nature", writes Maurizio Balsamo in "De l'origine" ["On the origin"] (2001, translated for this edition),

> could a point of absolute fixity be a junction between that history and its infinite transcriptions (despite attesting to the fact that a historical re-investment has taken place)? Could it be a point of paradoxical certainty, a condition related to a (psychotic) myth of the origin? (p. 766)

In agreement, I would add that this paradoxical certainty founds the possibility of survival—the possibility, that is, to confide in one's own psychotic capacity as an armour against all possible intrusions.

With regard to the origin, Aulagnier traces psychotic potential back to when "primary delusional thinking tries to reconstruct a missing fragment in the discourse of the Other" (2001, p. 174). What the other is missing can become the unique anchoring point for the construction of the self—something along the lines of: "where you end, I carry you on". In the psychotic dimension, one never stops having the other as a reference point—that is why, at the point where containment or missing the other ends, there psychotic expansion begins; and where the latter is contained, the other's containing presence begins.

Considering that psychosis is a vital necessity, the analyst's first objective cannot be to cure it or defend from it, rather to seek to entertain and take care of it. The analyst's difficulty resides in his desire of normality, effectively a wish to mould the other in his own image, whereas any contact with the psychotic dimension demands an unavoidable acknowledgment and, at the same time, annulment of every wish to change this essential and fragile core that needs preservative immobility.

Clearly, the psychotic patient (and, to a lesser degree, all other patients) would never tolerate being captured by the analyst and dragged into a transformational experience. The psychotic patient, in particular, cannot risk such an event, which would be devastating. Indeed, he can only contemplate the eventuality of a relationship where there is no apparent exchange and where the only active subject is himself. Costantino (2002) stresses that the worlds of the patient and therapist are essentially at odds with one another—one cannot come too close to the other without fear of losing himself. Psychotic expansion is an attempt to find an inner space that cannot be constructed, a locus where one can put and preserve one's objects. Psychosis concerns affects, thoughts, and ideas, which demand to be articulated and bound in an ever better-constructed form. These developments are particularly visible in the playing and the drawings of psychotic children.

Expansion of self-boundaries and integration in the analytic setting

When Cristina, a psychotic nine-year-old girl, whispers to me, "Cold as it is, of course I'm hot", the short phrase succinctly sums up the competitive nature of her relationship with the world. She can only be that which the world does not expect her to be. The words also conceal the tragedy of her origin and fate. Psychotic patients possess a strange knowledge, or display, at the very least, a form of thinking that constantly alludes to a vast knowledge. This is often evoked in the concise, enigmatic phrases they blurt out unexpectedly, often leaving one feeling inadequate. "You only eat the skin, I eat the skin and the meat", Cristina says to me once; might this mean there is something I do not understand and cannot contain, something that inevitably spills over and escapes me?

In his book, *Le visuel et le tactile: Essai sur la psychose et l'allergie* [The Visual and the Tactile: An Essay on Allergy and Psychosis], Sami-Ali proposes a definition of psychotic behaviour:

> In psychosis, the subject has no inner world, and psychopathology is essentially expressed through a massive use of projection. External and internal reality is the same thing. Everywhere, the subject is in the presence of another who is still himself. (1984, p. 20, translated for this edition)

One might also argue, however, that the psychotic's relationship to the other is more complex, as, alongside this lack of distance, there is also an attempt to distinguish oneself from the other. The psychotic, in fact, feels different from, and superior to, everyone else, and refuses to relinquish this omnipotence.

During our sessions, Cristina and I play catch. As she throws me the ball, she accompanies it with phrases and word games: "I'm a nomad", she says, "because I move towards the ball, while you stay sitting down." Her choice of the word "nomad" strikes me in particular—the term evokes an existence without a homeland or boundaries, a different way of being, eschewing self-definition and avoiding capture. It is precisely this lack of definition that becomes the affirmation and presence of the other's absence. In another game, Cristina places three toy cows inside a pen and comments, "This pen is for mad cows." The representation compresses a great capacity for tragedy and irony, as well as containment.

Cristina is six when she begins analysis with me, and has already had a prior experience of therapy. She was born prematurely and showed an autistic defence in her early years. In our first sessions, she is indifferent to all stimuli, as if entirely self-sufficient. She runs around the room, from one side to the other, with her hands in her mouth, emitting a hebephrenic laugh. An initial containment is possible through drawing and playing with plasticine. She asks me to draw her parents coming to pick her up, and then her as a boy, in the company of her father and the man she imagines to be my husband, whom she nicknames the "dancer-man". Once my tidy drawings are complete, she adds some extra touches to distort them. It is as if, from the outset, Cristina is asking me for an order in which to wreak her disorder. Over time, she begins to draw suspended, well-rounded figures, which she always marks with a dark stain. The obsessively dominant theme of her drawings is birth—a belly containing a baby girl, a mother. Coming to and leaving our sessions is dramatic for her; she almost always asks to see my navel and wants to show me hers.

A year into the therapy, Cristina's beginning school establishes a new boundary. She is much less standoffish and quiet, but experiences our separations even more dramatically—so much so, in fact, that one day she recites a kind of poem and makes me write it on the back of a drawing she has done "of an armless friend":

> Don't forget the days where we meet again
> don't spoil days by putting them in your mouth

I want to be more together
we must see each other every day
you must not say bye to my house
all children are happy and content
when we see each other.

At other times, she talks, or tells me stories, about her doll called Pitri, whose arms—like the figure in the picture—she has also removed. After her parents separate, one of these nursery rhymes about the doll seems obliquely to address the separation. "Pitri was a spiteful child. He wanted to be angry because he felt left out. Pitri cried because they weren't together any more, then they got together again and the next day he was happy and didn't feel left out any more. Pitri went to school to get everyone together and felt closer and closer next to them." This appears to be less a case of bringing together the parents in an oedipal sense than an attempt to avoid an uncontrollable expansion of self-boundaries, which would entail, as Sami-Ali suggests, an extreme dispersion of fragments of the self projected to family figures. This would explain the significance of the lack of arms: Cristina does not wish to remain armless, like her doll, having entrusted each parent with the functioning of one of her arms, the capacity of acting for her.

It is around this time that Cristina draws several pictures, which illustrate her more primitive needs. In the first (Drawing 1), she asks for my help in representing her father; next to him, on his right side, she draws a sick little girl. In Drawing 2, she depicts a fantasy of returning to the maternal womb with her mother. Drawing 3 represents her feelings of impotence. By always relating both joyful and painful events to dynamics in the relationship with her parents, Cristina seems to talk to me as if I were an other-self who should not only contain those events, but also articulate and join them together.

Cristina's subsequent drawings are somewhat different. She becomes the protagonist and begins to organise aspects that she previously projected and disseminated, which are now held together by the first significant ties. The change, which occurs at the beginning of her third year of therapy, coincides with an event that happened during the summer, when she and her cousin, who is slightly older than her, played games of a sexual nature. Her parents are terror-stricken and tell me about the episode as if it were an act of monstrous perversion,

Drawing 1.   Cristina's first drawing.

Drawing 2.   Cristina's second drawing.

Drawing 3.   Cristina's third drawing.

but Cristina had, in fact, already represented it in a series of drawings (Drawing 4). With their clear sexual connotations, the figures she depicts suggest that she had actually experienced the events in terms of a construction and working through of her internal world.

Through the experience, Cristina seems to have discovered that separate entities may desire one another and, therefore, strive to join together. In this first experience of desire, she had discovered a bond, which made it possible, consequently, to conceive of the relationship with an object. Of course, this experience was clearly a perverse one, but, none the less, it assisted her process of initial individuation and relationship with the other. By all accounts, it was the first time that she experienced intensely a relationship of the body, not of the mind.

Drawing 4.   The fourth drawing by Cristina.

In her following drawings Cristina represents two family scenes. The first, Drawing 5, depicts her "family at play", while Drawing 6 shows "Cristina with her father, whose head is in the clouds". Drawing 7, in which Cristina draws herself looking in the mirror, illustrates that, for the first time, she has contemplated the possibility of seeing herself or creating an image of herself.

Drawing 5.   Cristina's drawing of the family playing.

Drawing 6. Cristina and her father with his head "in the clouds".

Those aspects that, in all likelihood, represent schizo-paranoid splitting are now experienced as two expressions of the self. As the analytic containment allowed Cristina to promote her ego functions, the activity of drawing was no longer seen as an erratic projection of fragments of the self, but as the representation of what she herself contained, transformed into psychic experiences with which she could

Drawing 7.   Cristina's drawing of herself looking in a mirror.

identify. I believe this also allowed her to devote herself more fully to playing, as she seemed more capable of articulating meaning and symbolising gestures.

After these events, and alongside talk of birth and nutrition, Cristina manifests a tentative capacity for intentional and ego-driven aggressive behaviours. She begins to show hints of hostility and aspects of identity which represent a forcefulness that had always frightened her, and which, therefore, she tended to project, perhaps to not risk undermining the unity she was attempting to build. In the last session before the Christmas holidays, Cristina divides up all the toy animals in the consulting room, placing the good animals out on the table and putting the bad ones away in a basket. I suggest that today she wants to bring only the good things with her and leave the bad ones with me. She answers that on Monday we will play with all the animals of the forest. Then, holding a globe in her hand, she whispers that she is going to leave for Brazil and amuses herself by repeatedly telling me that she is never coming back. The words distress me somewhat, and I tell her that I do not want this to happen; she laughs and begs me to repeat the game over and over again.

While the first part of Cristina's therapy was entirely characterised by regression (behaving without restraint; leaping from one thing to the next; playing and speaking like a new-born child), at the end of the third year, the projective functioning and attendant self-boundary diffusion is compensated by efforts of containment.

In another of her drawings (Drawing 8), Cristina represents this self-boundary expansion in the form of pregnancy. On the left-hand side of the page, she draws herself lying down and heavily pregnant. In the picture, she is asked by another character how old she is, and, for the sake of realism, replies that she is thirteen years old, almost four years older than she actually is. The capacity for containment is represented both by the numerical age limit (she says she is thirteen and not, for example, fifteen) and the line of containment, which encircles and isolates the pregnant Cristina from the rest of the scene, and from which only the number thirteen escapes, as if to give an idea of futurity. Even her bulging belly is contained by a black band.

Approximately nine months later, Cristina adds another figure to the same picture, squeezed into the right-hand side of the page. It

Drawing 8.   Cristina's eighth drawing.

depicts the suffering analyst about to give birth, a pained expression of rejection on her face, and a smiling Cristina happily pushing on the analyst's belly to help the baby come out. The baby itself is first drawn, and then shaded over in black. She draws this picture before the summer break. What strikes me as truly unique is that, for the first time, our relationship is represented as inverted in relation to the past, and more appropriate to our present reality—there is a mother expecting a baby and a girl that recognises this. This role reversal, however, also bears another meaning: Cristina is performing a function of containment and support to the black ball, the small "black sun" in the analyst's belly.

I believe that, through transference, Cristina is able to represent the dynamics of the forces at play and, for the first time, also take on the vital aspects of her premature birth—taking responsibility for her mother's depression and bearing its burden. Typically, the psychotic patient has difficulty inhabiting the present and, thus, takes refuge in an imaginary and confused time.

One day, Cristina says to me, "I will not end at ten, I'll be twelve, fourteen, sixteen. At sixteen, I want a mother who always wants to stroke me." This fantasy is an attempt to maintain the split between a good experience and a bad one, between an object that can be kept and one that can be lost. Shortly after, she adds, "My mother always has a problem, always finds something to niggle about."

In more recent sessions, Cristina tells me about her past. She relates memories of the therapist she had in early childhood, along with recollections of when she first came to me, aged six, and the games we used to play together (catch, the "dancer-man", the pregnant monkey, Cristina and the baby's bottle, the village of animals, the globe, etc.). For the first three years of her therapy, Cristina also played a game of an entirely different nature, which we called the dreams game. At a certain point in the session, she would put the lights off and close the shutters, creating a nocturnal atmosphere, a kind of incubation or sacred place for sleep, like the ancient Greeks used to. She would then sit beside me, in the armchair behind the couch, wanting for us to tell each other our dreams. In this way, we sketched out a kind of "dream doodle", each of us influencing the other, to the point that often our narrations, tinged with imagination and fantasy, contributed to creating a single dream or delusion. In one session, Cristina was recounting her usual tales of narrow escapes from cruel monsters as I attempted to connect to her narrative through free associations that came to mind of my own childhood memories, when her words suddenly seemed to acquire particular significance for both of us. Cristina was telling me that she was in a dark forest, when she happened upon a tree next to which a squirrel was imprisoned, caught in a trap. Her father, who was on his way, would surely free it. I told her that, as a child, I often felt imprisoned by my mother, and that only my father could make me feel free. Cristina replied that this was precisely what she wanted to say with her dream.

In this instance, an area of complicity seemed to have been created, an intermediate space, which is the symbolic dreaming space. Kaës and colleagues state that the transitional function is born from the restoration of the capacity to articulate the symbols that join objects in the paradoxical playing space, beyond the constraints of division–separation or union–fusion (Kaës et al., 1979). The possibility of creating a transitional space for dreaming, provided by the relationship, allows the child to experience it not as a real, imprisoning event, but as a shared experience that is able to contain both emotionally and culturally. Cristina's dream illustrates the transition from an encapsulated, internal space to an area in which there is a deep emotional identification, and stages the appearance of a signifying third in the relationship with the analyst. This signifying third allows her to recognise the symbolic content of her dream. The analyst, in her countertransference experience, enhances the oneiric content of the child patient and allows it to be understood emotionally and articulated verbally through linguistic contamination. As Russo writes,

> In the unconscious, linguistic elements appear and are given meaning in relation to infantile experience, rather than from their insertion in the universal linguistic code. I have defined this unconscious process "original contamination" between language and things, without which there would be neither representations nor interpretations. By this process, all forms of textual construction and secondary elaboration of interpretation may begin. Linguistic contamination, therefore, makes up the raw material worked by the unconscious to move forward, creating verbal junctures with representations, secondary elaborations, and interpretations. (2005, p. 129, translated for this edition)

In another of our "oneiric encounters", Cristina tells me that she and her mother are held prisoners in a castle, when a knight suddenly arrives to free them. The theme of liberation is present once again, and I feel that I am the one held responsible for her imprisonment. I tell her that I dreamed of a very little girl; and she whispers that she dreamed of herself as a grown-up embracing this same little girl. The interweaving of our dreams momentarily allows Cristina to relinquish her internal split.

In some cases, it appears that reverie provides a way to enter children's dreams, and prevent them from vanishing. This interweaving can allow us to experiment with the importance of the dream within the context of the relationship, alongside the dream's meanings that we will be able to work through. In *Learning from Experience*, Bion writes,

> When the mother loves the infant what does she do it with? Leaving aside the physical channels of communication, my impression is that her love is expressed by reverie . . . The term reverie may be applied to almost any content. I wish to reserve it only for such content as is suffused with love or hate. Using it in this restricted sense reverie is that state of mind which is open to the reception of any "objects" from the loved object and is therefore capable of reception of the infant's projective identifications whether they are felt by the infant to be good or bad. In short, reverie is a factor of the mother's alpha-function. (1994, pp. 35–36)

The mother who is capable of reverie (i.e., who is endowed with the capacity to meet the child's psychic needs) is similar to the analyst who can come close to the latent dimension of the patient's dreams. The function of reverie is grafted on the psychotic core of the manifest dream and elicits the dream work.

Four years into the analysis, sessions with Cristina, who has turned ten, become primarily concerned with questions of memory and separation. With regard to the latter, Cristina does not identify with something separate, but, rather, with something that her object suddenly misses. Returning again to Drawing 8, one can see that Cristina has represented herself as the analyst's black hole. This is confirmed by the "farewell game", another of the games we play, in which Cristina leaves for good and I am left to weep inconsolably; she is happy to be what I miss, because, in this way, she is realising a paradox: "I exist when you miss me".

Over time, Cristina has built an order that includes a lack that cannot be filled or circumscribed, on which every relationship with the world hinges. She has been able to experience her own affective and ideational oscillations by modelling herself on the analyst's capacity to understand or reject her psychic content, and it is this modelling experience that she reproduces in her games and drawings. I would like to emphasise how essential the analyst's emotional responsiveness is in these case. Similarly, in consultations with Cristina's separated parents, whom I saw on a monthly basis, I felt it more important to listen rather than to offer hasty advice or interpretations. It seemed to me that, in so doing, what was being elicited was a warm disposition towards their little girl—who, with my mediation, could talk to them without blaming them any longer.

The onset of psychosis as ego containment

"Objects that you lose hurt at first."

(One of my young patients)

Childhood psychosis appears almost always to have the function of compensating for the fragility of the ego, which is still not adequate to conform to the demands of reality. We could, therefore, overturn the most widely accredited thesis according to which the ego is rendered fragile by the psychotic illness, and consider, instead, that the psychotic break tries to compensate ego fragility *vis-à-vis* reality. In this case, the psychosis would be a sort of narcissistic recovery, which juxtaposes delusion to the persecutory external reality. "Before the ego is constituted, giving meaning is not possible", writes Baldassarro (2004, pp. 1078–1079, translated for this edition),

> consequently psychosis, where the ego is somewhat constituted, would represent the ongoing failure of signification, which would explain the ceaseless wandering of the psychotic, as he is faced with the necessity and the impossibility to account for his origin, which drives him to look for a place that would give him hospitality and meaning.

When the mother–child relation has not developed in a "good-enough" way that could permit a happy transitional experience, the child finds himself in the condition in which he can neither be the mother, nor has the mother successfully been her child. This relational deficit causes a poverty of identifications and appropriate ego functions. The child's mind tries to make up for this fault through the psychotic onset, which is both an attempt to create an internal world to put in the place of the external reality and, at the same time, to withdraw from it.

The operation I have described, whose value is exquisitely economical, is a way to find an internal world in the external one, where the latter cannot be internalised, a way of expanding in the external space, to create transitory objects suited to the self, when the real objects have been unable to adapt sufficiently to the child's needs. Of course, in these cases the ego is "flooded"; however, in the psychotic episode, this is not always completely and immediately the case, and the ego is able to utilise its emerging psychotic contents to avoid the break when faced with an irreconcilable reality.

In one of our sessions, Cristina (whom I discussed above) once says, almost to herself, "Cold as it is, of course I'm hot", and this kind of oxymoron bespeaks her internal conflict. In a sense, with this construction of words, she is creating an asymmetric point of view on herself and her relations with the world. By asserting that her family environment is so emotionally cold, it is she who must do all the hard work, expand her self-boundaries, to provide warmth. In this way, she is also representing the type of relationship she maintains with her affective environment.

Psychotic children tend to create neologisms or utilise complicated words because reality and the language that articulates it do not correspond to what they want to say. Hence, unusual words or verbal constructions appeal to them particularly, insisting more on the signifier than the signified. As these children have not established the link between thing-presentation and word-representation, they give external legitimacy to their internal world of unconscious phantasies (which is not yet acknowledged as such) by creating combinations of words in play, whose meanings they are not always familiar with, in the hope that such words might become officially recognisable tools to bring objects back to them. For example, to evoke the idea of mental chaos, Cristina uses the word "hubbub", a type of noise that indicates both what she experiences outside and within herself.

And yet, alongside this, as I have suggested, psychotic children are endowed with a strange knowledge—a form of intuition or revelation of profound truths concerning both themselves and their objects. This is an endowment that far exceeds the capacity of an ego, which must inevitably renounce an aspect of the truth, in keeping the internal and external world differentiated and having to mediate between them. Where the ego is not, there the psychotic episode might well try to be.

When Giulia comes into therapy at six as a result of serious learning difficulties at school, I realise that her mind is entirely occupied by a single compulsive interest: delivering babies, as if this were the only way to dominate and control her trauma. Giulia has a brother who was born at the time of the onset of her psychosis. Alongside her concerns about defending herself from a trauma experienced passively, by trying to acquire an active role in the event Giulia also appears to be pursuing a therapeutic strategy that borrows its qualities from the trauma itself.

In the games she plays, which revolve around her delivering babies, certain details shed light on what is truly at play. First, Giulia becomes aroused and mimics a sexual act, as she makes one doll give birth to another; she then reveals that the babies being born are not whole babies, but only pieces of baby, and only later does she express an interest in putting all these pieces together to form a baby that is complete. This signifies quite clearly that, with the birth of her brother, Giulia had gone to pieces, and that her game strategically involves piecing children back together in order to rebuild her own self. The game also allows her to satisfy her desire to tear her brother to pieces, as well as all other potential brothers.

To these ends, Giulia digs out a large doll, about as big as her, from a closet at home and names her "Little giant". The doll clearly represents her body-self, to which she has turned to find some containment in the face of a disappointing reality. In other words, the subject uses the body as a primitive ego function—as body ego. The body is the first thing to regressively intervene and react in the onset of psychosis to defend from reality; indeed, it is not uncommon for infantile psychosis to be accompanied by metabolic disorders or organic diseases, which can, at times, be very serious.

Predictably, Giulia's body features very prominently in our sessions. In cases like these, the body presence could indicate that the child has had, at the very least, a good enough body relationship with the mother (hence, the only ego she can use to defend herself from trauma is the body ego); in another sense, however, this could also signal that the mother–child relationship has had little possibility of becoming a psychic one. An example of this might be the difficult process of transforming the first concrete bodily and drive manifestations into constructions that are progressively more and more symbolic.

"Little giant" is already a compromise between an inordinately large, material body and the possibility of using the doll as its symbolic equivalent. In the analysis, the transition was informed by my telling Giulia François Rabelais's story of Gargantua the giant. I used the story as a metaphor for the ego that needs to portray itself as imposing and very needy, just as the giant's size required him to be fed with so many litres of milk and be dressed with so many metres of fabric. It seemed to me that, precisely because Giulia liked the metaphor, facilitated as she was by her previous creation–invention of "Little giant", the experience would allow her to begin to recognise a symbolic level as sufficiently representative of the self.

Giulia's investment of the session was characterised by the intrusiveness of her aggressive body, but—to return to the case previously discussed—Cristina's expansion of self-boundaries was a more ideational and frankly delusional act. It is important to bear in mind that Cristina was born prematurely and had been placed in an incubator. Unlike Giulia, what Cristina was missing was a relational experience of the body—the relationship with her mother was, and remained, a prevalently mental one. At the beginning of the therapy, her need to show off her body indiscriminately had reached a point that worried me. These displays happened often, but the most emblematic was to show off her navel and want to press it against mine. For Cristina, this all seemed to occur without any emotion whatsoever, while for me it was very distressing. Her delusion, which essentially regarded body image and positioning in space, made her parents decide to take her to another therapist. They were very concerned about Cristina beginning school and, at the time, were still married but considering separating.

Cristina's being born premature had led her to preserve a considerable need for regression, while reality issued compelling requests that she grow up. In therapy, this need for attachment and the tension needed to establish a contact which could then perhaps give rise to a relationship was expressed through the creation of plasticine models, depicting her pregnant mother, crying children, and the full moon. Often she would burst into tears, for no apparent reason. I would observe that, when children cry, they want to be comforted, and she would sit on my lap and dry her tears. She once said that she cried for all the children and all the mothers who have lost their children, as if only mothers grieving for losing a child and only children grieving for having left their mothers could finally find a way of reuniting—as if only pain, guilt, and repentance could establish a bond.

My experience with Cristina made me reflect on how difficult it is to establish a relationship with the analyst that is not one of mutual dependence—the sole condition that can make the risk of a total dependency tolerable. This occurs, for example, with psychotic children who know they also have power over the analyst. I believe that this power can manifest itself in different ways, both in relation to the analyst's unconscious aspects (what we now often call "unanalysed residues") and when the analyst has a strong investment potential due to the need to find new libidinal objects after working through a loss (for example, patients who terminate analysis, or the departure or loss of a loved one).

Cristina switches from making plasticine models to drawing, the theme of pregnancy returning insistently to represent the imaginary events of the analytic relationship. To return again briefly to Drawing 8, we might surmise that the child is able to work through her dependence only by representing it in an identifiable and shared form, which also allows for role reversals. In the first part of the drawing, occupying the left-hand side of the page, the child is pregnant and the analyst is distracted by, or perhaps worried about, the precocity of the situation. An alternative interpretation could also be that it is, in fact, an oedipal rivalry that is upsetting the analyst's appearance in the drawing. In the second part of the drawing, added on the right-hand side of the page, it is the analyst who is pregnant—the pregnancy represented by the "black sun" she bears in her belly, which the little girl holds up and contains with evident happiness. The girl seems satisfied to be able finally to control the pregnancy from which she was prematurely expelled. It seems that, for Cristina, being pregnant means to be the depository of depression (see the black mouth, the black band around her belly, the "black sun" in the second picture) as if her personal history originated in the inheritance of her mother's depression after her premature birth, while the therapeutic situation could also permit the reverse path.

Both parts of the picture are pervaded by an intense core of pain, as depicted by the two black spots—one in the girl's mouth, the other in the analyst's belly. The trauma of birth has truly left its mark on Cristina's history; indeed, at one point during labour, both Cristina and her mother were in mortal danger. Even if life eventually prevailed, it had to fight against a strong death drive—against a tendency, in other words, to revert to a condition predating the pain that continues to be present in Cristina's representations of the world. It is significant to see how, in the relationship, the patient is able to carry over the pain from one person to the other.

Although Giulia's linguistic expression is very primitive, she almost always conveys some kind of meaning that may be shared, and I can avail myself of stories with which she can identify; Cristina's language, on the other hand, is entirely detached from reality. Even when she attempts to adhere to reality (coinciding, as this inevitably does, with the recognition of the other) she avoids shared meanings and creates parallel phrases deprived of all consequentiality. Since Cristina feels that the other's thinking will always overpower hers, she avoids the constructions and connections she associates with it, often using negation in place of assertion. She is afraid of being neutralised by the other's language because it is real, and, therefore, writes her own story, which only in certain moments of rebellion resonates in a manner that may be shared.

By way of example, I will reproduce a short text Cristina comes up with in order to communicate her anger at her father and me. Instead of taking her to the end of year party at her school, her father has brought her to the session, and she did not dare protest. We can see, through her acrobatic constructions, that Cristina succeeds in expressing a desire that is in conflict with someone else's, and to recognise the importance of this statement.

I was supposed to go to the party
Today is Thursday
I was supposed to come on Monday
When daddy came he answered me arrogantly and was wrong about
    there not being therapy
I was supposed to go to the party
But I couldn't go because I had therapy
Last time I had therapy
Not this time but seeing as he brought me here an excuse to waste
    time

Parents are also responsible for making their kids have fun
This is just an excuse to make me waste time
He stops bothering me only when I'm doing my homework
But not when there's the party
Daddy is wrong because he doesn't do anything constructive because
    he's always wrong
But when you have to go you have to go
He's not a child you have to protect yourself from but you have to
    answer him politely because he is daddy
I would have said "Let's go to therapy" to mum
But my father's different.

Of course, even these linguistic convolutions—originating from the child's psychosis and expressing its drama—have the power to contain the ego, to relate it to reality, to the child's history and desire. In a game Cristina enjoys very much, she repeatedly dials her father's phone number. When I suggest to her that perhaps she is angry with her father because he is not answering, she answers yes, not because this is necessarily the case, but because at that moment she has the impression of having grasped some sense of meaning, and, thus, appropriating an experience that previously eluded her.

Hence, it is not so much a question of getting hold of the truth of psychotic experience (which is split off and, therefore, unavailable to the subject) but, rather, of finding something plausible that can connect to the experience so as to give it a provisional meaning. For instance, if, during play, Cristina says that a little girl has been captured, she can only attribute responsibility for this to a policeman—a psychic agency that gives the event order and meaning. But, in her inner world, she sees only two alternatives for the girl—either getting lost or being captured; it is impossible for her to just be. The psychotic's modes of speaking (speaking nonsense or talking to themselves) are ways of protecting the ego from the dangers of being understood by others (i.e., of being captured by others).

Therapeutic factors in the treatment of psychosis

Over the foregoing pages, I have discussed some specific aspects and forms of the analytic relationship with psychotic patients. I hold that it is only possible to establish a relationship that can be configured as a mutual analyst–patient dependence, as this is the only way in which the psychotic patient can accept the risk of an almost complete dependence. In other words, a therapy whose primary task is to begin to integrate fragments of the ego has necessarily to go through the agony of dependence. In these vicissitudes, the need for a symmetrical relationship is inseparable from the therapeutic aims.

Lacan suggests that, at the beginning of a therapy with disturbed patients, the analyst turns himself into a scribe. And for Winnicott, too, the good-enough mother becomes invisible with her child, as Hernández and Giannakoulas have observed (2003). Returning to the issue of dependence, I believe that the human condition requires the subject to go through an experience of mutual dependence, like that between mother and child, or lover and loved one. Without this prior mutual dependence, attaining human subjectivity would be experienced as such a grievous trauma that it could not be worked through.

Drawing on my clinical experience, I have attempted to define the main factors in psychoanalytic psychotherapy with difficult patients. In the relationship with psychotic patients, I think this principally resides in the work carried out by the analyst's ego—a labour that should not necessarily be put to the patient, but that is thought and worked through, and, thus, contained and held by the analyst. This therapeutic attitude partly concerns the capacity for reverie, or the ego's availability to receive something not yet formed, which is different from the ego itself and its function of anticipation. This mode of functioning tends to reorganise the ego of the analyst, her identifications, projections, and defences, so as to be able to accept and, later, to understand and give meaning to the oneiric–delusional fragments seeking to be integrated through a new experience. In short, this is an experience of simultaneous deconstruction and reconstruction of the ego—first of all, the analyst's, and, consequently, the patient's.

On a visit to the Ovetari Chapel in Padua, I was once able to admire early restoration work on Andrea Mantegna's Renaissance frescoes in the Eremitani Church. The Chapel was bombed during the Second World War, and these masterpieces were left in fragments; the restoration workers were reassembling the frescoes' thousands of disordered particles, like pieces of a puzzle. We could apply this idea of the fragmented body one tries to reassemble to the psychotic patient, to the state of fragmentation and possible reconstruction of his self and his world. But things are not that simple with psychotic patients, because one has the impression most of the time that there is no underlying drawing to be reconstructed—it is a matter, instead, of configuring something entirely new, with no reference to an existing past. In a sense, we could say that the psychotic patient ejects fragments that are not the broken pieces of a drawing, but serve to fill the partial void left by the object. Yet, we know that what feels empty also contains the compulsion to repeat something, albeit something painful. One wonders, therefore, whether another important therapeutic factor might be the analyst's willingness to be pliable, to allow himself to take part in that repetition, and be able to tolerate it in spite of the tension it creates internally, so that it can provide the building blocks for the construction of the subject's ego. In fact, it is always important to rely on the subject's potentials and developmental drive, however lacking the original object might have been.

In my first session with Cristina, the little girl races around the room screaming that she has seen a mouse. When these hallucinations and screams subside, she talks confusedly about a mouth. I connect this terrified race around the room to her fear of oral greed. The scene is perturbing, and I first react with fantasies of rejection of Cristina, which I dare not acknowledge, even to myself, because I feel sorry for her, and perhaps also a sense of solidarity (something we often feel because we have something in common with someone). To attract Cristina's attention, but also to take my mind off my own thoughts, I begin to play with a piece of plasticine. When Cristina becomes aware of this, she takes it perhaps as an invitation or as openness on my part, and picks up the piece of plasticine and begins to shape it into amorphous objects. It seems possible, then, to hypothesise that my early rejection could be linked not so much to the violence of her greed (which is certainly disquieting, particularly when we become aware that we, too, could be the object of such greed) but, rather, with the fear of the formlessness with which I was in danger of identifying.

This experience was significant for both of us and laid the foundation for the following seven years of work. I believe the idea of using plasticine, being able to touch something material—almost corporeal —was a productive and spontaneous intuition, allowing us to locate our mutual shapelessness in a shared object so as to begin to represent it. In the analytic relationship with the psychotic, the analyst, as far as possible, must not differentiate from the subject, to get close to the patient's sensory mode of functioning. The psychotic must be able to shape the analyst to their needs.

The mother as environment and the mother as object that Winnicott writes about are so intrinsically contained in the needs of the subject that the therapist must always take this into account when responding to the patient's transference. In *The Non-Human Environment in Normal Development and Schizophrenia* (1960), Searles argues that the development of symbolic thinking is one of the factors that allow the psychotic to break free from his previous identification with the non-human world. The non-human environment initially protects the subject from the persecutory object and from his hatred of such an object, but it also forces him to remain in a mode of relating in which his identifications marginalise him from language.

As her therapy progresses, Cristina uses plasticine to create a world that has not yet acquired a definitive form, but a provisional and transitory one, before moving on to express herself with drawings. A few years later, she stages the birth of a monkey puppet followed by the birth of a doll (as described above), and this becomes a regular activity. Cristina's play shows how she repeatedly attempts to stage the differences between her and me, while needing to preserve some equivalence between us, as she tries to understand these differences.

After this experience of differentiation, and having reached puberty, Cristina begins to talk with less confusion about her family history and in clearer terms about her difficult relationships with her peers. As she grows gradually more able to articulate her thoughts and differentiate time and space, her true pain emerges. Although she rarely speaks to me about dreams, she narrates a dream that strikes me as emblematic, in which she is standing upside down on a spiral staircase and is terrified. What does the patient wish to represent with this dream? Was it the fear of not yet being born? Or fear of the world from which she sought shelter, through the regressive act of descending the staircase? (And was this linked to Freud's preceding moment, perhaps? Or the psychotic's fear of regression theorised by Searles?)

In one of our most recent sessions, Cristina takes a sheet of paper and draws a picture of herself and a boy called Gabriele, whom she has never mentioned before. She tells me that after the session she will go and see Gabriele. When I ask who Gabriele is, she tells me he is a problematic child who attended the same primary school as she did (Cristina is now in the first year of secondary school). Because of his difficulties, she tells me, Gabriele's mother took him out of the school, and the same happened with another girl, Monica. According to her version of events, she seemed to be the only pupil to have successfully completed primary school.

I realise that years must have passed since Cristina last saw this Gabriele. Does she have his telephone number, I ask? Cristina writes the number on a sheet of paper and I recognise her father's phone number, missing a zero. I remark that to desire something and to not be able to have it is very difficult to bear. Cristina looks at me intensely and asks what desire is; I answer that it is missing that which we do not have. I can sense Cristina's difficulties in leaving the retreat of her closed world to enter another one.

Cristina's mode of thinking appears to characterise a process of narcissistic withdrawal in psychotic patients, which is similar to dream work: as soon as a wish is felt, it is displaced to an equivalent object that is more similar to the self. This object already exists detached from reality in one's own world, so it is possible to think that the wish, which the ego is catching glimmers of, has, in fact, already been realised. To put it differently, instead of the psychotic patient's absence of repression freeing the ego to address deeply unconscious contents, the ego receives such contents in a disguised form similar to the dream form. This still constitutes a delusion, even if in very attenuated form. The psychotic has had hardly any experience of going beyond the self, and, for this reason, he tries to remain enclosed within an autarchic world, which he imposes upon himself from the beginning.

Psychoanalytic work with psychotics entails an intense effort to reduce the grandiose self, and a continuous attempt to surpass what was alive and has been congealed. Although the symbolic world might be difficult to reach, it is always possible to encounter an imaginary world with some good objects.

CONCLUSIONS

"**D**ifficult" is a fitting adjective for the identities that this book describes, in the sense, too, that my own experience with these patients has often felt like a taxing, hindrance-ridden journey, if only for the resistances on both sides of the analytic couple, which are always at work both during analysis and in writing about it.

Every time a feature of identity gains consistency, this always entails a work of separation. This is always painful for the therapist as well, whether she has loved or hated the aspects of the self contained in the patient and with which she can now identify. Then again, this process is certainly the most therapeutic possible, in the sense that it relieves psychic suffering, because it leads to the transformation of internal objects (see Chapter Three) through identifications and projections that go on all the time both in the patient and analyst.

Significantly, Freud mentions the word "identity" only once in *The Interpretation of Dreams* (1900a), in discussing the notion of "perceptual identity". This concept addresses the transition of the psychic apparatus from a chaotic to a well-formed and orientated dimension. After the breach of biological homeostasis, bodily needs activate the drives that look for an object; initially, however, the drives are chaotic forces precisely because they have not yet found an object. Freud puts forward the hypothesis that, after the first experiences of satisfaction, the psychic apparatus moves towards a perceptual identity, which functions as a code for the regulation of the psychic apparatus itself.

To my mind, the analytic relationship proceeds along similar lines. In the early stages, both the patient and the therapist move toward one another psychically (for example, the use of plasticine with Cristina), like the mouth and the nipple trying to meet for the first time. Only after a while, when both have acquired a perceptual identity, can they know how to proceed affectively to be able to meet.

However, the therapeutic relationship is, at the very least, nourished by an incipient transference that acts as a compass for guiding the earliest chaotic steps, which can be thought about only when the encounter takes place. The transferential engagement is initially unconscious for both parties, and the experienced therapist can feel its emotional impact, though it is not yet available for conscious thinking. I also believe that when transference is established, the construction of identity has already begun, and, therefore, new portions of the ego have been formed. In other words, when some transference signs reach conscious awareness, this means that certain deeper, unfulfilled aspects of the patient and analyst have already met, giving rise to the work of representation that occurs in both members of the couple. When the couple attains the capacity to represent, which manifests itself in the implicit and readily interpretable equivalents of consciousness (dreams, drawings, stories), we are already getting to know a portion of the ego, and two provisional identities face one another.

This process is certainly easier to observe in young children, but years of clinical experience have trained my eye for it in adolescents as well. I am convinced that almost all children and adolescents who are in analysis need to carry out the work of identity (i.e., to reorganise, construct, or put it to the test), because they are deeply troubled by their dependence on others without whom they cannot function— either because they are too young or because they are struggling to establish an adult autonomy. Whenever it is possible to have a satisfactory experience in the therapeutic relationship (through play, or drawing, or some equivalent activity, akin to dreams and verbalisation) a psychic experience has been constituted, and the patient can identify with it and, at the same time, gain a degree of separateness. Thus, each piece of the analytic experience functions as a building block towards the construction of identity, as well as a bit of mourning work.

"Integration starts right away at the beginning of life", writes Winnicott, "but in our work we can never take it for granted" (2001a, p. 150). By entrusting the analyst with everything he knows about himself, Winnicott argues, the patient already seems to trust that, in time, the analyst will assemble all of his pieces together: "To be known means to feel integrated at least in the person of the analyst".

When, for example, Pietro (see Chapter Nine) cries at being left in my consulting room by his father, I draw him and his father together, and the itinerary from their home to my consulting room, and he is able to appropriate what is going on and is reassured. Although it might be tempting to attribute these sorts of phenomena to empathy, I would relate them to unconscious identifications mobilised by mutual transference, within the context of what Winnicott calls a relationship of transitional development (2005a). Many such experiences would thus accrue so that the subject is finally able to construct the object with whom to identify.

Nadia's dream (see Chapter Seven) provides a similar example. If the jar of low-calorie jam can signify many things, one of them is certainly the patient's need to communicate her way of being "nourished"—with extreme caution, that is, and without an excessive desire to feed or the aggression that comes with seduction. But if Nadia is able to have this dream, it is because she has had enough experiences of the therapist to be able to trust that this event can be represented.

With both Pietro and Nadia, the unconscious fit between patient and therapist—which can become conscious—already signals the existence of a constructive relationship of transference and countertransference. To return, in conclusion, to the question of identity, I shall discuss briefly Bolliger and Capek's fairytale, *The King and the Flute Player*. The story, which I will paraphrase, goes something like this.

Once upon a time there was a king. Asleep in his royal bed one night, the king had a dream. In his dream he saw a tree, and on top of the tree sat a bird. The bird was singing a beautiful song.

When he awoke the next day, the king summoned the bird-catcher and told him, "I had a dream last night. I saw a tree, and on top of the tree sat a bird singing a beautiful song. I want you to go and catch that bird for me!"

"Yes, my king!" replied the bird-catcher. "What kind of bird was it?" But the king said he did not know. "Just go and catch it", he commanded. "I will give you seven days."

The bird-catcher was frightened of the king's anger. So he took his flute and his bird-catching net and went out into the gardens. He hid behind a wall, whipped out his flute, and played the song of the black-bird. When the blackbird left its nest, he caught it in his net, put it into a cage, and brought it to the king. "No", the king said, "That's not the right bird."

On the second day, the bird-catcher took his flute and his bird-catching net and went out into the fields. He hid behind a hedge, whipped out his flute, and played the song of the lark. When the lark left its nest, he caught it in his net, put it into a cage, and brought it to the king. "No", the king said, "That's not the right bird."

On the third day, the bird-catcher took his flute and his bird-catching net and went out to the stream. He hid behind a stone, whipped out his flute, and played the song of the golden oriole. When the golden oriole left its nest, he caught it in his net, put it into a cage, and brought it to the king. "No", the king said, "That's not the right bird."

On the fourth day, the bird-catcher took his flute and his bird-catching net and went out to the woods. He hid behind a tree, whipped out his flute, and played the song of the song thrush. When the song thrush left its nest, he caught it in his net, put it into a cage, and brought it to the king. "No", the king said, "That's not the right bird."

On the fifth day, the bird-catcher took his flute and his bird-catching net and went out to the edges of the forest. He hid behind a bush, whipped out his flute, and played the song of the wren. When the wren left its nest, he caught it in his net, put it into a cage, and brought it to the king. "No", the king said, "That's not the right one."

On the sixth day, the bird-catcher took his flute and his bird-catching net and went out into the park. He hid behind a fountain, whipped out his flute, and played the song of the nightingale. When the nightingale left its nest, he caught it in his net, put it into a cage, and brought it to the king. "No", the king said, "That's not the right bird."

On the seventh day, the bird-catcher had run out of all the bird-songs he knew how to play. He decided it was useless to hide, and walked to the king's palace. He took out his flute and played his own song. "This is the last time I will ever play my song", he thought to himself as he played. "The king will surely throw me in prison and take my flute away."

The bird-catcher played more beautifully than he ever had before. The king, who was having breakfast in the palace, put down his knife and fork. "That's the song!" he cried out. "That's the song I heard in my dream!"

He summoned the bird-catcher at once. "Where is the bird?" he asked. "That's not a bird," the bird-catcher replied, "that's my own song". The king was astonished. To show how very pleased he was, he called for huge celebration. All the birds were set free from their cages, and the bird-catcher was given his freedom once more.

In the story, recognition of identity begins with an experience of satisfaction and encounter with the other, and the desire of the other elicits the desire of self. Indeed, the king and the bird-catcher's mutual recognition is the construction of the matrix of identity, while the bird-catcher's journey represents the subject's intimate search for self-expression and fulfilment through a sense of aliveness and freedom. Together, patient and analyst carry out the work of identity in a similar way, taking it in turns to be the desiring subject and the satisfying object. The king, like the child, has a wish but does not know yet which object can satisfy it. And the bird-catcher, like the mother, makes several attempts to realise that wish—that is, to give the child the imagined object which only then can become a reality and, thus, give real satisfaction.

One thing that strikes me about the story is that it is only when the bird-catcher is able to give himself that he succeeds in coinciding with the desire of the other. The work that precedes the realisation—wandering through many different places (the unknown), looking for many birds (the many facets of desire)—recalls the difficulty that every human being faces when constructing a sense of identity.

All the young patients discussed in these pages, who needed to find or strengthen their identities, were able to do so through their emotions and the analyst's, and with the assistance of play, drawings, and words; they eventually succeeded in recovering the maternal function that they had repudiated out of anger or resentment, and engaging their paternal function, which could help them separate from the original matrix with which they had reconciled themselves. The young adolescent patients have also gone through a similar process of transformation, accepting within their sexual identity the pleasure of recognising themselves in their own bodies, thanks to the analyst who—as an adult—can see their potential for adulthood. Like the king, who represents infantile omnipotence and frees the bird-catcher, thus the child can let go of the mother when he reaches the capacity to identify with her on whom he depended to acknowledge his desire. What psychotherapists await is precisely to be released when the other feels free. To be recognised and therefore succeed in appropriating one's destiny might well be a good end to a successful analysis.

Hans in luck

Jacob and Wilhelm Grimm,
translated by D. L. Ashliman (2002)

H ans had served his master for seven years, so he said to him, "Master, my time is up. Now I would like to go back home to my mother. Give me my wages."

The master answered, "You have served me faithfully and honestly. As the service was, so shall the reward be." And he gave Hans a piece of gold as big as his head. Hans pulled his handkerchief out of his pocket, wrapped up the lump in it, put it on his shoulder, and set out on the way home. As he went on, always putting one leg before the other, he saw a horseman trotting quickly and merrily by on a lively horse.

"Ah", said Hans quite loud, "what a fine thing it is to ride. There you sit as on a chair, never stumbling over a stone, saving your shoes, and making your way without even knowing it."

The rider, who had heard him, stopped and called out, "Hey there, Hans, then why are you going on foot?"

"I must", answered he, "for I have this lump to carry home. It is true that it is gold, but I cannot hold my head straight for it, and it hurts my shoulder."

"I will tell you what", said the rider. "Let's trade. I will give you my horse, and you can give me your lump."

"With all my heart", said Hans. "But I can tell you, you will be dragging along with it."

The rider got down, took the gold, and helped Hans up, then gave him the bridle tight in his hands and said, "If you want to go fast, you must click your tongue and call out, 'jup, jup.'"

Hans was heartily delighted as he sat upon the horse and rode away so bold and free. After a little while he thought that it ought to go faster, and he began to click with his tongue and call out, "jup, jup". The horse started a fast trot, and before Hans knew where he was, he was thrown off and lying in a ditch which separated the fields from the road. The horse would have escaped if it had not been stopped by a peasant, who was coming along the road and driving a cow before him.

Hans pulled himself together and stood up on his legs again, but he was vexed, and said to the peasant, "It is a poor joke, this riding, especially when one gets hold of a mare like this, that kicks and throws one off, so that one has a chance of breaking one's neck. Never again will I mount it. Now I like your cow, for one can walk quietly behind her, and moreover have one's milk, butter, and cheese every day without fail. What would I not give to have such a cow?"

"Well," said the peasant, "if it would give you so much pleasure, I do not mind trading the cow for the horse." Hans agreed with the greatest delight, and the peasant jumped upon the horse and rode quickly away.

Hans drove his cow quietly before him, and thought over his lucky bargain. "If only I have a morsel of bread—and that can hardly fail me—I can eat butter and cheese with it as often as I like. If I am thirsty, I can milk my cow and drink the milk. My goodness, what more can I want?"

When he came to an inn he stopped, and to celebrate his good fortune, he ate up everything he had with him—his dinner and supper—and all he had, and with his last few farthings had half a glass of beer. Then he drove his cow onwards in the direction of his mother's village.

As noon approached, the heat grew more oppressive, and Hans found himself upon a moor which would take at least another hour to cross. He felt very hot, and his tongue stuck to the roof of his mouth with thirst. "I can find a cure for this", thought Hans. "I will milk the cow now and refresh myself with the milk." He tied her to a withered tree, and as he had no pail, he put his leather cap underneath, but try as he would, not a drop of milk came. And because he was working in a clumsy way, the impatient beast at last gave him such a blow on his head with its hind foot, that he fell to the ground, and for a long time did not know where he was. By good fortune a butcher just then came along the road with a pushcart, in which lay a young pig.

"What sort of a trick is this?" he cried, and helped good Hans up. Hans told him what had happened.

The butcher gave him his flask and said, "Take a drink and refresh yourself. The cow will certainly give no milk. It is an old beast. At the best it is only fit for the plough, or for the butcher."

"Well, well", said Hans, as he stroked his hair down on his head. "Who would have thought it? Certainly it is a fine thing when one can slaughter a beast like that for oneself. What meat one has! But I do not care much for beef, it is not juicy enough for me. But to have a young pig like that! It tastes quite different, and there are sausages as well."

"Listen, Hans", said the butcher. "To do you a favour, I will trade, and will let you have the pig for the cow."

"God reward you for your kindness", said Hans as he gave up the cow. The pig was unbound from the cart, and the cord by which it was tied was put in his hand. Hans went on, thinking to himself how everything was going just as he wished. If anything troublesome happened to him, it was immediately set right.

Presently he was joined by a lad who was carrying a fine white goose under his arm. They greeted one another, and Hans began to tell of his good luck, and how he had always made such good trades. The boy told him that he was taking the goose to a christening feast. "Just heft her", he added, taking hold of her by the wings. "Feel how heavy she is. She has been fattened up for the last eight weeks. Anyone who bites into her after she has been roasted will have to wipe the fat from both sides of his mouth."

"Yes", said Hans, hefting her with one hand, "she weighs a lot, but my pig is not so bad either."

Meanwhile the lad looked suspiciously from one side to the other, and shook his head. "Look here", he said at last. "It may not be all right with your pig. In the village through which I passed, the mayor himself had just had one stolen out of its sty. I fear—I fear that you have got hold of it there. They have sent out some people and it would be a bad business if they caught you with the pig. At the very least, you would be shut up in the dark hole."

Good Hans was terrified. "For goodness' sake", he said. "Help me out of this fix. You know more about this place than I do. Take my pig and leave me your goose."

"I am taking a risk," answered the lad, "but I do not want to be the cause of your getting into trouble." So he took the cord in his hand, and quickly drove the pig down a bypath. Good Hans, free from care, went homewards with the goose under his arm.

"When I think about it properly," he said to himself, "I have even gained by the trade. First there is the good roast meat, then the quantity of fat which will drip from it, and which will give me goose fat for my bread for a quarter of a year, and lastly the beautiful white feathers. I will have my pillow stuffed with them, and then indeed I shall go to sleep without being rocked. How glad my mother will be!"

As he was going through the last village, there stood a scissors grinder with his cart, as his wheel whirred he sang, "I sharpen scissors and quickly grind, / My coat blows out in the wind behind."

Hans stood still and looked at him. At last he spoke to him and said, "All's well with you, as you are so merry with your grinding."

"Yes", answered the scissors grinder, "this trade has a golden foundation. A real grinder is a man who as often as he puts his hand into his pocket finds gold in it. But where did you buy that fine goose?"

"I did not buy it, but traded my pig for it."

"And the pig?"

"I got it for a cow."

"And the cow?"

"I got it for a horse."

"And the horse?"

"For that I gave a lump of gold as big as my head."

"And the gold?"

"Well, that was my wages for seven years' service."

"You have known how to look after yourself each time", said the grinder. "If you can only get on so far as to hear the money jingle in your pocket whenever you stand up, you will have made your fortune."

"How shall I manage that?" said Hans.

"You must become a grinder, as I am. Nothing particular is needed for it but a grindstone. Everything else takes care of itself. I have one here. It is certainly a little worn, but you need not give me anything for it but your goose. Will you do it?"

"How can you ask?" answered Hans. "I shall be the luckiest fellow on earth. If I have money whenever I put my hand in my pocket, why should I ever worry again?" And he handed him the goose and received the grindstone in exchange.

"Now," said the grinder, picking up an ordinary heavy stone that lay nearby, "here is another good stone for you as well, which you can use to hammer on and straighten your old nails. Carry it along with you and take good care of it."

Hans loaded himself with the stones, and went on with a contented heart, his eyes shining with joy. "I must have been born with lucky skin", he cried. "Everything I want happens to me just as if I were a Sunday's child."

Meanwhile, as he had been on his legs since daybreak, he began to feel tired. Hunger also tormented him, for in his joy at the bargain by which he got the cow he had eaten up all his store of food at once. At last he could only go on with great difficulty, and was forced to stop every minute. The stones, too, weighed him down dreadfully, and he could not help thinking how nice it would be if he would not have to carry them just then.

He crept like a snail until he came to a well in a field, where he thought that he would rest and refresh himself with a cool drink of water. In order that he might not damage the stones in sitting down, he laid them carefully by his side on the edge of the well. Then he sat down on it, and was about to bend over and drink, when he slipped, pushed against the stones, and both of them fell into the water. When Hans saw them with his own eyes sinking to the bottom, he jumped for joy, and then knelt down, and with tears in his eyes thanked God for having shown him this favour also, and delivered him in so good a way, and without his having any need to reproach himself, from those heavy stones which had been the only things that troubled him.

"No one under the sun is as fortunate as I am", he cried out. With a light heart and free from every burden he now ran on until he was at home with his mother.

REFERENCES

Algini, M. L. (2003). *Il viaggio con i bambini nella psicoterapia* [*The Psychotherapeutic Journey with Children*]. Rome: Borla.

Algini, M. L., & De Silvestris, P. (1992). Percorsi di occultamento [Itineraries of concealment]. *Quaderni di psicoterapia infantile, 24*: 217–229.

Anzieu, A., Anzieu-Premmereur, C., & Daymas, S. (2000). *Le jeu en psychothérapie de l'enfant* [*Playing in Child Psychotherapy*]. Paris: Dunod.

Aulagnier, P. (2001). *The Violence of Interpretation: From Pictogram to Statement*, A. Sheridan (Trans.). Hove: Routledge.

Azar, A. A. (1997). Le bon usage du "matrimoine" en psychopathologie [About the good use of "matrimony" in psychopathology]. *Adolescence, 29, 15*(1): 287–298.

Baldassarro, A. B. (2004). Sull'originario nella psicosi [On the originary in psychosis]. *Rivista di Psicoanalisi, 50*(4): 1077–1096.

Balsamo, M. (2001). De l'origine [On the origin]. *Revue Française de Psychoanalyse, 65*(3): 757–777.

Bernhard, T. (2010). *Gathering Evidence: A Memoir*, D. McLintock (Trans.). New York: Vintage.

Bion, W. R. (1994). *Learning from Experience*. Lanham, MD: Rowman & Littlefield.

Blixen, K. [Dinesen, I., pseud.] (1963). *Ehrengard*. London: Michael Joseph.

Blixen, K. [Dinesen, I., pseud.] (1987). *On Modern Marriage and Other Observations*, E. Cederborg (Ed.), A. Born (Trans.). London: Fourth Estate.

Bollas, C. (1989). The destiny drive. In: *The Christopher Bollas Reader* (pp. 37–56). London: Free Association Books.

Bolliger, M., & Capek, J. (1986). *Das schönste Lied*. Zürich: Bohem Press.

Bonaminio, V. (1993). On not interpreting: two clinical fragments and some considerations for a reappraisal of M. Balint. *Rivista di Psicoanalisi (English edition)*, *39*: 69–92.

Borges, J. L. (2011). *The Book of Sand and Shakespeare's Memory*, A. Hurley (Trans.). London: Penguin.

Brabant, E., Falzeder, E., & Giampieri-Deutsch, P. (Eds.) (1993). *The Correspondence of Sigmund Freud and Sándor Ferenczi: 1908–1914*. Cambridge, MA: Harvard University Press.

Catherine of Siena, Saint (2008). *The Letters of Catherine of Siena (Volume 4)*, S. Noffke (Ed. & Trans.). Tempe, AZ: Medieval and Renaissance Texts and Studies.

Chianese, D. (2006). *Un lungo sogno* [*A Long Dream*]. Milan: FrancoAngeli.

Costantino, O. (2002). La parola e la psicosi [The word and psychosis]. *Psicoterapia Psicoanalitica, 9,1*: 10–26.

Cupelloni, P. (Ed.). (2002). *La ferita dello sguardo* [*The Gaze's Wound*]. Milan: FrancoAngeli.

Deutsch, F. (Ed.). (1959). *On the Mysterious Leap from the Mind to the Body: A Workshop Study on the Theory of Conversion*. Madison, CT: International Universities Press.

Dolto, F. (1979). *The Jesus of Psychoanalysis: A Freudian Interpretation of the Gospel*. Garden City, NY: Doubleday.

Dostoevsky, F. (2004). *The Adolescent*. New York: Vintage.

Faimberg, H. (2005). *Telescoping of Generations: Listening to the Narcissistic Links Between Generations*. London: Routledge.

Ferenczi, S. (1932). The confusion of tongues between adults and children: The language of tenderness and of passion. *International Journal of Psychoanalysis, 30*: 225–230.

Ferenczi, S. (1980). The dream of the clever baby. In: *Further Contributions to the Theory and Technique of Psycho-Analysis* (pp. 349–350). New York: Brunner–Mazel.

Ferrari, A. (2004). *From the Eclipse of the Body to the Dawn of Thought*. London: Free Association.

Foscolo, U. (1808). *Dei Sepolcri, poesie di Ugo Foscolo di Ippolito Pindemonte e di Giovanni Torti*. Piacenza: Dai Torchi del Maino.

Freud, A. (1967). About losing and being lost. *Psychoanalytic Study of the Child*, 22: 9–19.

Freud, S. (1895). *The Project for a Scientific Psychology. S. E., 1*: 281–387. London: Hogarth.

Freud, S. (1900a). *The Interpretation of Dreams. S. E., 4–5*. London: Hogarth.

Freud, S. (1905d). *Three Essays on the Theory of Sexuality. S. E., 7*: 123–246. London: Hogarth.

Freud, S. (1911b). Formulations on the two principles of mental functioning. *S. E., 12*: 213–226. London: Hogarth.

Freud, S. (1914c). On narcissism: an introduction. *S. E., 14*: 67–104. London: Hogarth.

Freud, S. (1915b). Thoughts for the times on war and death. *S. E., 14*: 273–300. London: Hogarth.

Freud, S. (1917e). Mourning and melancholia. *S. E., 14*: 237–260. London: Hogarth.

Freud, S. (1920g). *Beyond the Pleasure Principle. S. E., 18*: 1–64. London: Hogarth.

Freud, S. (1923b). *The Ego and the Id. S. E., 19*: 1–66. London: Hogarth.

Freud, S. (1924c). The economic problem of masochism. *S. E., 19*: 155–172. London: Hogarth.

Freud, S. (1927c). *The Future of an Illusion. S. E., 21*: 1–56. London: Hogarth.

Freud, S. (1933a). *New Introductory Lectures on Psycho-Analysis. S. E., 22*: 1–182. London: Hogarth.

Freud, S. (1937c). Analysis terminable and interminable. *S. E., 23*: 209–254. London: Hogarth.

Giannakoulas, A. (1999). Corteggiamento, innamoramento, amore e genitorialità [Courtship, falling in love, love, and parenthood]. In: A. Nicolò Corigliano (Ed.), *Curare la relazione: saggi sulla psicoanalisi e la coppia* (pp. 33–52). Milan: FrancoAngeli.

Green, A. (1996). *On Private Madness*. London: Karnac.

Grimm, J., & Grimm, W. (2002). Hans in luck, D. L. Ashliman (Trans.). www.pitt.edu/~dash/grimm083.html (accessed 16 January 2018).

Guillaumin, J. (1997). Expérience esthétique et identité [Aesthetic experience and indentity]. *Adolescence, 15*(1): 19–31.

Gutton, P. (1991). *Le pubertaire* [*The Pubertal*]. Paris: PUF.

Gutton, P. (2002). *Psicoterapia e adolescenza* [*Psychotherapy and adolescence*]. Rome: Borla.

Haddon, M. (2012). *The Curious Incident of the Dog in the Night-Time*. London: Vintage Books.

Hernández, M., & Giannakoulas, A. (2003). Sulla costruzione dello spazio potenziale [On the construction of potential space]. In: M. Bertolini, A. Giannakoulas, & M. Hernández (Eds.), *La tradizione winnicottiana* (pp. 101–118). Rome: Borla.

Hinshelwood, R. D. (1994). *Clinical Klein*. London: Free Association Books.

Hugo, V. (1856). *Les Contemplations*. Paris: Nelson éditeurs.

Kaës, R., Missenard, A., Kaspi, R., Anzieu, D., Guillaumin, J., & Bleger, J. (1979). *Crise, rupture et dépassement* [*Crisis, Rupture and Beyond*]. Paris: Dunod.

Klein, M. (1927). Criminal tendencies in normal children. *British Journal of Medical Psychology, 7*: 177–192.

Klein, M. (2017)[1940]. Mourning and its relation to manic-depressive states. In: *The Collected Works of Melanie Klein (Volume I)* (pp. 344–369). London: Karnac.

Kluzer Usuelli, A. (1992). The significance of illusion in the work of Freud and Winnicott: a controversial issue. *International Review of Psycho-Analysis, 19*: 179–187.

Kristeva, J. (1995). The adolescent novel. In: *New Maladies of the Soul*, R. Gubberman (Trans.) (pp. 135–153). New York: Columbia University Press.

Lacan, J. (2003). *Family Complexes in the Formation of the Individual*. Chippenham: Anthony Rowe.

Laplanche, J. (1989). *New Foundations for Psychoanalysis*. Oxford: Blackwell.

Manzano, J., Palacio Espasa, F., & Zilkha, N. (2001). *Scenari della genitorialità* [*Scenarios of Parenthood*]. Milan: Raffaello Cortina.

Mascagni, M. L. (1995). Studiare Winnicott [Studying Winnicott]. *Psicoterapia Psicoanalitica, 3*(1): 133–146.

Masciangelo, P. M. (1988). Su Freud per il dopo Freud. Una riflessione metapsicologica [Concerning Freud for the after-Freud: a metapsychological reflection]. In: A. Semi (Ed.), *Trattato di psicoanalisi (Volume 1)* (pp. 395–474). Milan: Cortina.

McGuire, W. (Ed.) (1974). *The Freud/Jung Letters: The Correspondence Between Sigmund Freud and C. G. Jung*. Princeton: Princeton University Press.

Merleau-Ponty, M. (1968). *The Visible and the Invisible*, C. Lefort (Ed.), A. Lingis (Trans.). Evanston, IL: Northwestern University Press.

Plato (2008). *Symposium*, R. Waterfield (Trans.). Oxford: Oxford World's Classics.

Pontalis, J.-B. (1981). *Frontiers in Psychoanalysis: Between the Dream and Psychic Pain*. London: Hogarth Press.

Pontalis, J.-B. (1988). *Perdre de vue* [*Losing from Sight*]. Paris: Gallimard.

Recalcati, M. (1997). *L'ultima cena: anoressia e bulimia* [*The Last Supper: Anorexia and Bulimia*]. Milan: Bruno Mondadori.

Romano, L. (1979). *Una giovinezza inventata* [*An Invented Youth*]. Turin: Einaudi, 1995.

Russo, L. (2005). Autoanalisi ed interpretazione [Self-analysis and interpretation]. In: P. De Silvestris & A. Vergine (Eds.), *Consapevolezza e autoanalisi: strategie di approssimazione all'esperienza inconscia* (pp. 116–140). Milan: FrancoAngeli.

Sami-Ali, M. (1984). *Le visuel et le tactile: Essai sur la psychose et l'allergie* [*The Visual and the Tactile: An Essay on Allergy and Psychosis*]. Paris: Dunod.

Schacht, L. (1988). La planète imaginaire. De l'utilisation de l'aire intermédiaire dans la phase initiale d'une psychothérapie d'enfant [The imaginary planet]. *Journal de la Psychanalyse de l'Enfant, 5*: 235–262.

Schulz, B. (1990). *Letters and Drawings of Bruno Schulz: With Selected Prose*, J. Ficowski (Ed.), W. Arndt (Trans.). New York: Fromm International.

Searles, H. F. (1960). *The Non-Human Environment in Normal Development and Schizophrenia.* New York: International Universities Press.

Searles, H. F. (1994). *My Work With Borderline Patients.* Oxford: Rowman & Littlefield.

Thanopulos, S. (2005). Leonardo's phantasy and the importance of Freud's slip: the role of the analyst's phantasies in applied psychoanalysis and in the analytic relation. *International Journal of Psychoanalysis, 86*: 395–412.

Tolstoy, L. (1985). *The Kreutzer Sonata and Other Stories*, D. McDuff (Trans.). London: Penguin Books.

Tolstoy, L. (2016). *Anna Karenina*, R. Bartlett (Trans.). Oxford: Oxford World's Classics.

Wedekind, F. (2007). *Spring Awakening*, J. Franzen (Trans.). New York: Faber & Faber.

Weil, S. (2002). *Gravity and Grace*, E. Crawford & M. von der Ruhr (Trans.). London: Routledge.

Weil, S. (2004). *The Notebooks*, A. Wills (Trans.). Abingdon: Routledge.

Winnicott, D. W. (1965)[1960]. The theory of the parent–infant relationship. In: *The Maturational Processes and the Facilitating Environment: Studies in the Theory of Emotional Development* (pp. 37–55). London: Hogarth Press.

Winnicott, D. W. (2001a)[1945]. Primitive emotional development. In: *Collected Papers: Through Paediatrics to Psychoanalysis* (pp. 145–156). London: Routledge.

Winnicott, D. W. (2001b)[1949]. Birth memories, birth trauma, and anxiety. In: *Collected Papers: Through Paediatrics to Psychoanalysis* (pp. 174–193). London: Routledge.

Winnicott, D. W. (2001c)[1950]. Aggression in relation to emotional development. In: *Collected Papers: Through Paediatrics to Psychoanalysis* (pp. 204–218). London: Routledge.

Winnicott, D. W. (2005a). *Playing and Reality*. London: Routledge Classics.

Winnicott, D. W. (2005b). Mirror-role of mother and family in child development. In: *Playing and Reality* (pp. 149–159). London: Routledge Classics.

Winnicott, D. W. (2005c). Contemporary concepts of adolescent development and their implications for higher education. In: *Playing and Reality* (pp. 186–203). London: Routledge Classics.

INDEX